GREAT CAMPAIGNS

The Boston Campaign

GREAT CAMPAIGNS

THE BOSTON CAMPAIGN

April 1775 - March 1776

Victor Brooks

COMBINED PUBLISHING
Pennsylvania

PUBLISHER'S NOTE

The headquarters of Combined Publishing are located midway between Valley Forge and the Germantown battlefield, on the outskirts of Philadelphia. From its beginnings, our company has been steeped in the oldest traditions of American history and publishing. Our historic surroundings help maintain our focus on history and our books strive to uphold the standards of style, quality and durability first established by the earliest bookmakers of Germantown and Philadelphia so many years ago. Our famous monk-and-console logo reflects our commitment to the modern and yet historic enterprise of publishing.

We call ourselves Combined Publishing because we have always felt that our goals could only be achieved through a "combined" effort by authors, publishers and readers. We have always tried to maintain maximum communication between these three key players in the reading experience.

We are always interested in hearing from prospective authors about new books in our field. We also like to hear from our readers and invite you to contact us at our offices in Pennsylvania with any questions, comments or suggestions, or if you have difficulty finding our books at a local bookseller.

For information, address:
Combined Publishing
P.O. Box 307
Conshohocken, PA 19428
E-mail: combined@combinedpublishing.com
Web: www.combinedpublishing.com
Orders: 1-800-418-6065

Cataloging-in-Publication data available from the Library of Congress.

ISBN 1-58097-007-9

Maps by Paul Dangel
Printed in the United States of America.

Contents

Maps

Sidebars

CHAPTER I

The Gathering Storm

*D*uring the rainy, cold afternoon of Thursday, December 16, 1773, a crowd of over 7,000 people, almost half the population of Boston, filled Old South Meetinghouse to its capacity and swirled around surrounding streets. As sextons began lighting candles against the growing darkness, Samuel Adams stood on a pew in the front of the church and uttered a single sentence that would hurl the colonies toward war with Great Britain. Adams had just conferred with Francis Rotch, a 23-year-old Quaker from Nantucket who was part owner of the merchant ship *Dartmouth*, currently moored at nearby Griffin's Wharf. The ship's cargo hold was filled with 114 chests of East India Company tea. Rotch had just been informed by Royal Governor Thomas Hutchinson that, despite the protest of the citizens of Boston, the ship would not be permitted to return to England until the cargo was unloaded and the three pence a pound tax on tea was duly paid by the owners. When Rotch returned to Old South from his meeting with the governor it was nearly 6 P.M. and the tension was clearly mounting throughout the building. When the young merchant informed Adams that Hutchinson had refused to grant a pass, the veteran patriot leader rose and with a quavering voice announced, "This meeting can do nothing more to save the country."

At that moment, a war whoop came from the gallery of the meetinghouse and 40 or 50 men who had been lurking near the church door burst inside dressed as Indians, shouting war cries and exciting the crowd into a frenzy. Voices yelled "The Mohawks are coming!" "Hurrah for Griffin's Wharf!" "Boston Harbor's a teapot tonight!" and citizens began pouring out of the building as patriot leader John Hancock admonished them, "Every man should do what is right in his own eyes."

While most of the people attending the extraordinary meeting of a loosely defined organization called "the body" simply drifted to the dockyards to see what would happen next, about 150 men had much more specific plans. One group adjourned to newspaper publisher Benjamin Edes' house and broke out stocks of blankets and tomahawks reserved for the occasion; a second group met at the home of a merchant on Fort Hill and dabbed on homemade "war paint" while they practiced grunting to sound like Indians; a third contingent gathered at clockmaker James Brewer's house on Summer Street and enjoyed a wide variety of refreshments while Brewer's wife helped blacken men's faces with burnt cork while making comments about how fierce the "Indians" now looked.

By about 7 P.M., just as the afternoon rain was giving way to a clear, cold moonlit night, three groups of about 50 men each marched to Griffin's Wharf and boarded the vessels *Dartmouth*, *Eleanor* and *Beaver* which among them carried about 90,000 pounds of tea worth perhaps one million dollars in modern American currency. Each party of "Mohawks" boarded an assigned ship, demanded keys to the cargo holds from the senior officer present, and requested candles to illuminate their activities. On each ship, men began attaching block and tackle to the chests of tea and hoisted them from the hold while all other cargo was scrupulously left untouched. The now brilliant moon illuminated a scene of furious activity as over 300 chests of the "wicked brew" were pulled from the cargo holds by one group of "Indians," split open with axes by a second contingent and tossed overboard by a third unit. The tide was so low at this point that the water was only between two and three feet deep and the tea started piling so high on top of the water that it was drifting back onto the decks and had to be shoveled over again. Few words were spoken during the entire procedure and the men were so well disguised that spectators, including a sprinkling of pro-British Loyalists, had no real idea who was actually dumping the tea into the harbor. Paul Revere was probably the most well-known patriot leader who was actually aboard the ships that evening as John Hancock, Sam Adams and other notables were apparently merely watching from the wharf with other bystanders.

The whole operation was so covered with secrecy that one participant did not admit his role in the operation until 1847 when he was a robust 93 years of age, and another "Mohawk" came forward in 1848 at age 113.

The disguised patriots worked feverishly because a few hundred yards away a British naval squadron rode at anchor with enough firepower to blast the "Mohawks" and their supporters into oblivion. Admiral John Montagu, commander of the British warships, admitted that he refrained from giving orders to his ships to open fire due to the fear of causing horrendous casualties among the spectators. The admiral himself spent the evening playing cards at the home of a prominent Tory who lived only a few hundred yards from Griffin's Wharf. Montagu watched the whole operation with a mixture of bemusement and disdain and when the "Indians" marched away from the wharf, the admiral raised a window sash and yelled, "Well boys, you have had a fine, pleasant evening for your Indian caper, but mind, you have got to pay the fiddler yet." One of the patriot leaders, Captain Kendall Pitts, shouted back "Oh never mind! Just come out here if you please and we'll settle the bill in two minutes."

In a little more than two hours, the participants in the Boston Tea Party had dumped 342 chests of tea worth just over £9,000 into Boston Harbor. There was so much tea drifting around the water that the harbor took on the eerie appearance of an alien landscape. The brew shaped into dunes that blocked the sea lanes and clogged the harbor so much that sailors had to row out to churn the heaps of brown leaves away from the main ship channels. Tea was still spread for miles around the next morning when Paul Revere mounted a fast horse and started to carry the news of the exciting events as far away as New York and Philadelphia. His dispatches included a statement from the Boston Sons of Liberty to their counterparts in other colonies that "We are in a perfect jubilee, not a Tory in the whole country can find the least fault to the proceedings." As patriots in each town read Revere's reports, bells began to ring and colonists sent back messages of solidarity with their Boston comrades.

The Boston Tea Party was the culmination of a dispute between Britain and her American colonies over the legality of ministerial taxation that had been festering since parliament introduced the Stamp Act in 1765. While colonial opposition had waxed and waned as the British government introduced new taxes and then withdrew or reduced them, the main spark that set the fuse of armed conflict occurred when the ministry approved a plan to dump part of 18 million pounds of East India Company tea currently moldering in London warehouses on the American market. Parliament passed the Tea Act of 1773 which placed the lucrative American tea market in the hands of a few favored merchants while maintaining a universally unpopular three pence a pound tax on the beverage as it was imported into the colonies. One of the results of this legislation was that tea distribution in Massachusetts would be limited to five principal outlets, three of which were owned by Governor Hutchinson's relatives and the other two by long-time family friends. Patriot leaders emphasized that the dispatch of the tea ships from England to America presented two intolerable challenges to colonial autonomy. First, allowing the vessels to be unloaded after paying the tea tax would admit parliamentary right to tax Americans. Second, permitting the British government to decide who could legally sell tea in the colonies could easily be expanded to dozens of other commodities which would eventually lead to economic strangulation for any American businessman or merchant who did not have the right friends in London. Thus, if the tea was allowed to be landed on

American soil, the days of colonial autonomy would seem to be numbered. Thus when the "Mohawks" in Boston responded to this direct challenge by dumping the hated tea in the harbor, each side correctly saw the event as a watershed in the history of Britain's rule over the colonies and as a clear prelude to military confrontation between parliament and the American provinces.

On January 20, 1774, John Hancock's ship *Hayley*, which had left Boston on December 22, arrived in England with accounts of the Boston Tea Party which were almost immediately printed in London newspapers. When the destruction of the tea was brought up in parliament, even traditional friends of American autonomy exploded in fury. Colonel Isaac Barre denounced the tea party as an intolerable challenge to British rule in the colonies and Benjamin Franklin, then residing in London, wrote of "a great wrath sweeping the country" against Massachusetts and its lawless citizens. General Thomas Gage, commander of British forces in North America, was home in England on leave and was quickly closeted with King George III who sought his advice on the proper response to the event. Gage took an exceptionally hard-line approach as he advised his sovereign that "they will be lions while we are lambs, but if we take the resolute part, they will undoubtedly prove very meek."

The monarch encouraged his ministers to take a hard line against the Massachusetts provincials, and the result of this attitude was parliamentary passage of a series of bills collectively known as the Coercive Acts in Britain and the Intolerable Acts in America. The legislation effectively closed the port of Boston to most ships, moved the capital of Massachusetts to Salem, limited town meetings to a frequency of only once a year, nullified much of the original charter of the colony, and allowed the quartering of British troops in a variety of public and private buildings at the discretion of the senior military commander. Governor Hutchinson was recalled to England for "consultations" while General Gage was given a dual appointment as royal governor of Massachusetts and captain general of British military forces in the colonies, an action that teetered on the brink of turning Boston into an occupied city ruled by martial law.

On May 13, 1774, General Gage arrived in Boston Harbor and spent the next several days aboard ship conferring with Hutchinson and other local Tory officials. Four days later the new governor stepped ashore on Long Wharf escorted by a company of elite local militiamen commanded by John Hancock. Gage reviewed several militia units, attended an elegant dinner in his honor, and then retired to his office in Province House to initiate the mechanism of closing Boston Harbor when the Port Bill went into effect on June 1. Gage

Paul Revere's famous engraving of the Boston Massacre, March 5, 1770. Aside from the buildings, the print is surprisingly inaccurate. Respectable citizens are being shot on a sunny day by troops wearing uniforms discontinued in 1768.

noted that despite the surface cordiality of his welcome, there was a strong undercurrent of rebellion that terrified the "friends of government" in the city. "Many are impatient for the arrival of the troops and I am told that people will then speak and act openly where they now dare not do." At this point Gage's effective military force consisted only of a few companies of the 64th and 65th regiments of foot based in Castle William out in Boston Harbor while only politically unreliable provincial militia units were deployed in the town proper. Reinforcements were already on their way, but on June 1 when Boston Harbor was officially closed to shipping, the only significant British presence in the city was Admiral Samuel Graves' naval squadron which moved ominously to block entry to the port as the town's church bells tolled continuously through the streets of a now economically distressed community.

While Gage spent most of the next two weeks looking anxiously out of his office window for any sign of rebel military activity, on June 14 the 4th Regiment of Foot, the King's Own, arrived from Ireland and marched through the town to Boston Common where the troops pitched long rows of white tents. The next day the redcoats were joined by the 43rd Regiment of Foot, while on July 4 Lord Hugh Percy arrived in Boston with the 5th and 38th regiments. The transports that had delivered Percy's men to the town set sail to convey the 59th Regiment down from Halifax and the 23rd Regiment, the Royal Welsh Fusiliers, up from New York City. Gage had confidently assured his sovereign that he could enforce the Port Act with only four regiments of Regulars but almost as soon as he arrived in Boston he began to upgrade his estimate of required troops and orders were soon being issued on the far side of the Atlantic for substantial reinforcements to be sent to Massachusetts. By Christmas of 1774 the garrison in Boston proper had expanded to three reinforced brigades, including Lord Percy's 1st Brigade consisting of the 4th, 23rd and 47th regiments supported by a battalion of Royal Marines; Brigadier General Robert Pigot's 2nd Brigade deploying the 5th, 38th and 52nd regiments; and the 3rd Brigade which had not yet received a commander but included the 10th, 43rd and 59th regiments. This

Howard Pyle's 19th-century interpretation of the Boston Massacre adds accurate details such as snow, Crispus Attacks, and a more ruffian crowd, but the British troops are still depicted in outmoded uniforms.

imposing force was supported by elements of the 64th and 65th regiments stationed in Castle William and a newly arrived detachment of Royal Artillery that pushed the entire force of Regulars in Boston to just under 3,000 men, well over double the force that Gage had insisted would be sufficient the previous spring.

As Gage began consolidating his regiments into brigades, he also initiated a series of operations designed to overawe the local population with the strength of the British army while simultaneously reducing the military capabilities of the provincials. The first operation was authorized soon after William Brattle, a Tory-sympathizing general in the Massachusetts provincial militia, quietly informed Gage that the towns around Boston were gradually withdrawing their supplies of gunpowder from the main regional magazine, the Middlesex County Powder House on Quarry Hill near Cambridge. Early on the morning of September 1, 1774, Colonel George Madison, commanding officer of the 4th (King's Own) Regiment of Foot, gathered together a hand-picked force of 260 men selected from all of the British regiments. At 4:30 A.M. the detachment marched quietly to Long Wharf and boarded 13 longboats manned by naval personnel. The coxswains guided the vessels across Boston Harbor to the Mystic River and landed the redcoats at Temple's Farm. The troops quickly formed up and marched just under a mile to Quarry Hill where they were met by the sheriff of Middlesex County, Colonel David Phips, another Tory militia officer. Phips carried the keys to the windowless stone structure that housed the colonial powder supply, and within a few minutes redcoats were unloading 250 half barrels of powder from the storehouse. Meanwhile, Madison sent a small detachment over to Cambridge where they commandeered two brass field pieces that belonged to the province. By late morning, the troops were back in Boston and the munitions were safely deposited in Castle William, far out of the reach of the colonists.

Gage's raid had eliminated a substantial portion of the provincials' available powder, but the action also very nearly started a war. Accounts of the British operation were soon crisscrossing the roads and lanes of the colony with fact and rumor becoming hopelessly intermingled. One version insisted that six colonials had been killed in the area around Quarry Hill and that the King's ships were even then bombarding the city of Boston. All day long church bells tolled, and by nightfall fire beacons constructed decades earlier to warn of a French invasion were being lit to signal a threat from the former protectors from Britain. Towns as far away as Concord and Shrewsbury began mobilizing militia companies and by the morning of September 2, the countryside was swarming with men headed for Boston. A young traveler riding in the Massachusetts countryside that morning noted that "all along the road were armed men rushing forward, some on foot some on horseback. At every house women and children were making cartridges; they left scarcely half a dozen men in a town, unless old and decrepit, and in one town the landlord said he himself was the only man left."

The Connecticut Valley alone apparently sent nearly 20,000 men marching toward Boston "in one body armed and equipped" and this impressive array of manpower was over halfway towards its destination before messengers informed them that no blood had been spilled. The Reverend Ezra Stiles estimated that over one-third of the males in Massachusetts between the ages of 16 and 65 had been mobilized between September 1 and September 2, and he believed that 60,000 men could have ringed Boston by the morning of September 3 if the raid on Quarry Hill had actually cost provincial lives. At this point in time about half of Gage's authorized garrison was still in transit which would have forced the royal governor to attempt to hold Boston with fewer than 1,500 Regulars opposing almost 50 times their number in provincial militiamen. However, the British general dismissed reports of the "Powder Alarm" mobilization as being grossly exaggerated and quickly went back to planning even larger operations designed to disarm the colonists before they could develop into a major threat to the British garrison.

While Gage began fortifying Boston and planning new expeditions into the countryside, the Massachusetts patriots began making their own preparations for a clash of arms that now seemed increasingly likely. When the royal governor canceled the session of the General Court that was scheduled to be held in the new capital of Salem on October 4, 1774, patriot leaders accused Gage of attempting to run the colony without a legislature and promptly organized a Provincial Congress that began meeting at Concord on October 5. One of that body's first official acts was to initiate a takeover of the militia infrastructure of the province. First, the legislature directed that one-quarter of all eligible males in the colony would be recruited into companies of 50 privates and 3 officers "who shall equip and hold themselves in readiness on the shortest notice from the committee of safety to march to the place of rendezvous." These newly designated "minutemen" would be supplied with a bayonet, pouch, knapsack and 30 rounds of cartridges and balls and be disciplined at least three times a week in formal training activities. Meanwhile, the Congress began purging the rolls of the province militia officers of "ministerial sympathizers," a list which included two of the senior gen-

British reinforcements arrive in Boston in 1768. Long Wharf is at left.

erals in the colony, Timothy Ruggles and William Brattle. The legislature in effect abolished all current commissions in the militia and ordered the election or appointment of a new slate of officers in every town throughout Massachusetts. Thus by the end of 1774 the province could field an army of almost 40,000 men commanded by officers whose primary allegiance was to the Massachusetts Congress rather than to any superior in London. Ousted leaders such as Ruggles and Brattle quickly began to recruit a parallel "home guard" of Loyalist colonials, but the initial campaign was fairly disappointing as the only sizeable unit was a 200-man regiment raised in Boston. There were still a fair number of Loyalists in the Massachusetts countryside, but too few in any single community to form units large enough to actively challenge their patriot neighbors. When these Loyalist "friends of government" began informing Gage of the size and determination of what were now being called "rebel" forces, the British commander jettisoned his original optimistic estimate that four regiments could maintain British rule in Massachusetts and asked his superior in London for the astounding total of 20,000 reinforcements merely to hold Boston and its adjoining towns.

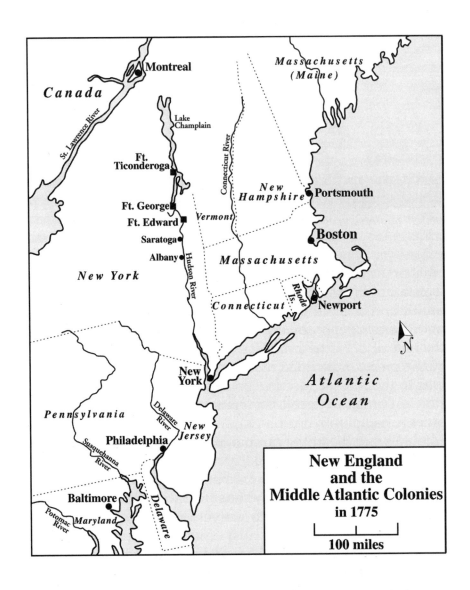

New England
and the
Middle Atlantic Colonies
in 1775

100 miles

Prime Minister Lord Frederick North and his minister for the American colonies, William Legge, Earl of Dartmouth, were startled by their commander's change of heart but did not entirely dismiss his reasoning. The British ministers agreed to provide Gage with a fairly large reinforcement, although well under the 20,000 requested, but it would be impossible to embark largely unseaworthy troop transports until sometime in the spring of 1775. The ministers agreed to send to Boston three additional British warships that would provide the naval squadron with extra firepower and also to cram the vessels with 700 additional Royal Marines. Since Dartmouth calculated Gage's current effective strength at 2,800 men, this reinforcement would produce an army of 3,500 redcoats by early spring. Once the weather along the sea lanes improved, Gage would also receive four additional infantry regiments, a regiment of cavalry, ten more companies of Royal Marines and 500 new recruits who would be used to fill out the rosters of regiments already stationed in Boston. This additional increment of about 3,500 men would provide the British commander with just under 7,000 men by June of 1775 with an assumption that at least 3,000 Loyalists could be recruited to provide a 10,000-man army for a summer offensive which would sweep the rebels from virtually every community in the Bay province.

Ironically, while the general was granted at least part of his request for reinforcements, the tone of his request sounded so shrill to North and Dartmouth that the ministers began to convince themselves that Gage was not the man for the job of suppressing an incipient rebellion in one of His Majesty's most valuable colonies. North's first preference was to convince Sir Jeffrey Amherst, one of the heroes of the French and Indian War, to accept command of all British forces in the Americas. Amherst was regarded as a hero by most colonists yet he actually detested America and its inhabitants and wanted no part of ever campaigning in the New World again. Amherst even bluntly rejected the king's personal request to assume command and North and Dartmouth were forced to settle for the temporary expedient of sending Gage three senior-level subordinates, William Howe, Henry Clinton and John Burgoyne while they evaluated the command situation in Massachusetts.

While his superiors plotted his replacement, Thomas Gage took stock of his available units and began considering the most effective way to employ his still rather limited resources. One of the general's most immediate concerns was that the battle experience that made the British Regular so feared in combat was largely absent in his Boston garrison. The Royal Welsh Fusiliers was an elite regiment that had seen extensive action in the Seven Years War, and the 5th Northumberland Fusiliers had also served with distinction on the Continent, but most of the remaining regiments had seen little, if any, serious combat. The 4th Regiment of Foot, the King's Own, had a glorious history and had been a vaunted force in several 17th-century campaigns but had sat out the Seven Years War garrisoning the West Indies along with the 38th and 64th regiments. The 10th Regiment of Foot had spent the last 20 years as a garrison force in Ireland while, ironically, the 18th Royal Irish Regiment had spent the same period camped in England. Most of Gage's other regiments were new units made up of raw recruits who probably had less military training than most units in the Massachusetts provincial army. Only the 47th Regiment of Foot had ever seen extensive service in America during the French and Indian War, and thus only a tiny fraction of the British garrison had either the training or the experience to prepare them for a conflict in the hills and forests of the colonial countryside.

Gage developed two possible remedies for this difficult situation. First, the army would engage in frequent firing exercises while light infantry companies would be repeatedly drilled in "Indian-style bush fighting," in which units would deploy as skirmishers along the line of march of the rest of the regiment and then fire blank powder charges at simulated enemies closing in on the column. These elite troops were also expected to practice reloading their weapons lying on their stomachs in the grass and to be prepared to maximize the advantages of concealment and cover. Second, the commanding general initiated a regular rotation of marches into the coun-

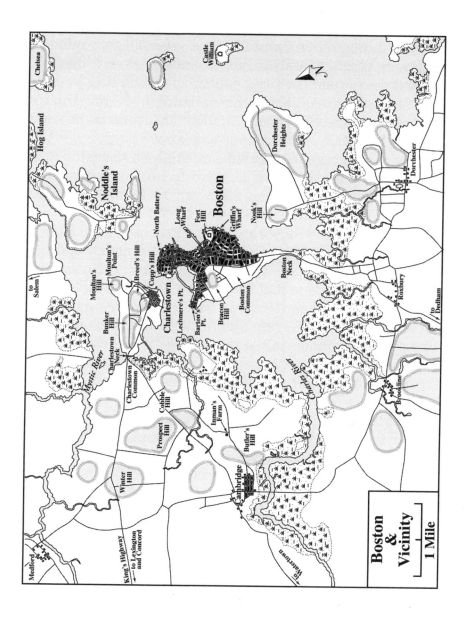

Boston & Vicinity

1 Mile

tryside in which regiments would march out to Brookline, Newton, Dedham or Waltham, conduct simulated battles to awe the "country people," and then march back to Boston by a different route while officers made special note of possible colonial strongpoints or ambush sites. While Gage would continue to be plagued by an inability to fully appreciate the fighting abilities of the provincial militia, he at least had the good sense to realize that armed confrontation in North America was not very likely to parallel battle maneuvers on the continent of Europe.

Gage's aggressive patrolling and high profile battle drills not only prepared his own men for future combat but also convinced the patriot leaders that war was imminent and that provincial military units must be organized as quickly as possible for conflict with the British Regulars. The Provincial Congress responded by naming a commanding general and four lieutenants to direct the Massachusetts army. The new commanding general was Jedidiah Preble, a 67-year-old veteran of the French and Indian War who was to be assisted by Artemus Ward, Seth Pomeroy, John Thomas and William Heath who were all veterans of the same conflict. While all of these men possessed a reasonable amount of talent and military experience, they were also collectively a rather old group of field commanders. Seth Pomeroy was nearly 80 years old and none of the new generals was much below 50, an advanced age by 18th-century standards. Preble promptly refused the offered command, and the position fell on Artemus Ward, who would be plagued by a number of painful ailments during most of the crucial first year of the war and seldom displayed the energy required of a successful field commander. Thus while key political leaders such as John Hancock, Joseph Warren and John Adams were relatively young men, the military fate of the Massachusetts provincials was placed in the hands of a group of men who would be either retired or in peripheral commands when the war reached its climax six years later.

When Artemus Ward assumed command of the provincial army, he was already a member of the powerful Committee of Safety which was effectively directing the military buildup throughout the colony. Ward and his fellow committee members correctly surmised that Gage's most likely targets in a full-scale military expedition would be the provincial magazines at Worcester, 47 miles from Boston, and Concord, 22 miles from the city. However, all during the fall of 1774 and the winter of 1775 wagons groaning with military supplies continued to rumble into the two towns as Ward and his colleagues became convinced that their numerous spies in Boston would provide ample warning of a British offensive. Unfortunately for the patriots, they did not realize that one of their most trusted members, Dr. Benjamin Church, was a spy for the British and was keeping Gage apprised of almost every aspect of patriot war plans.

Using Church's steady stream of intelligence as a basis for his strategy, Gage decided to send scouts to the two provincial supply depots to ascertain the advantages and drawbacks of large scale raids on Concord or Worcester. In January of 1775, the commanding general asked for volunteers from among those officers "capable of taking sketches of a coun-

Province House, headquarters of the British royal governor in Boston.

try." This cryptic request initiated speculation in the British camp about the purpose of the memorandum and also accentuated one glaring weakness in the officer corps. Lt. Frederick McKenzie noted sourly, "I am afraid not many officers of the army will be qualified for this service. It is a branch of military education too little attended to, or sought, by our officers, and yet is not only extremely necessary and useful in time of war, but very entertaining and instructive." At least two officers, Captain William Brown and Ensign Henry de Berniere, presented themselves to Gage with the requisite talents and on February 23 the men embarked on an adventure that would finalize much of Gage's operational strategy for the first campaign of the war. The two British officers, disguised as surveyors, crossed over the ferry from Boston to Charlestown accompanied by Corporal John Howe who was disguised as their servant. The scouts walked through Charlestown Peninsula, made careful observations of Breed's Hill and Bunker Hill, crossed Charlestown Neck, and headed for Cambridge. Their cover story as surveyors didn't last past their first rest stop. The three men stopped at Brewster Tavern for a meal, and Jonathan Brewster, a former member of the elite Rogers' Rangers, quickly identified the upper-class accents of the two "surveyors" as belonging to British officers. Then one of Brewster's serving girls, a young black woman who had recently left Boston, recognized the men as members of Gage's officer corps. When de Berniere casually remarked about the "fine country around here," the young waitress quickly retorted "it is a very fine country and we have many fine and brave men to fight for it. If you travel much further, you will find it to be true."

The three young Englishmen spent the next several days sketching possible marching routes and ambush sites on the road to Worcester while receiving both shelter and vital intelligence from local Tories who dotted the countryside. During an overnight stay in a Loyalist-owned tavern in Framingham, the soldiers were given a room which overlooked the town common which was currently being used by three companies of local militia who were obviously preparing for imminent hostilities. They overheard the militia's commander, Captain

Simon Edgell, emphasize the experience of most of the officers in the French and Indian War and noted his emphasis that "Americans are equal to the best troops in the world." The enthusiasm and energy of the officers and men greatly impressed the British Regulars who carefully noted these events in their official report. When Loyalist sympathizers in Worcester were unable to get the Englishmen into the main supply depot, the men used the cover of a late winter blizzard to slip back into Boston where they provided a grateful commanding general with reports, sketches and maps of the countryside.

Three weeks later the trio was asked by Gage to undertake a similar scouting mission to Concord and the expedition produced another round of secret meetings with local Tories and uncomfortable, and possibly dangerous, encounters with patriot patrols. One of the leading citizens of Concord, Daniel Bliss, was an ardent Loyalist who had collected extensive information on the local supply depot and provided detailed intelligence to the British officers. Bliss mapped out the location of 14 cannons, huge caches of cartridge boxes, powder, muskets, flints and entrenching tools, and noted that Colonel James Barrett's nearby farm was being used as an auxiliary magazine. When Bliss attempted to show the officers some of the patriot hiding places, the men were discovered and left Concord just as patriot patrols were converging to capture them. De Berniere informed Gage that "the road to Lexington is very open and good for six miles—but the following five miles are enclosed by hills and include several places that could afford an enemy good cover."

Bliss had provided the British with excellent intelligence concerning patriot supplies at Concord, but Gage seemed to waver between that town and Worcester as the target for his first offensive. Finally, the general ordered Lt. Colonel Francis Smith, commander of the 10th Regiment of Foot, to disguise himself as an itinerant laborer and scout the approaches to Worcester from the perspective of an expedition commander. On April 5, accompanied by the ubiquitous Corporal Howe, Smith trudged out of Boston and headed for Worcester. The whole concept of sending Smith on this mission bordered on complete farce. The British colonel was significantly over-weight and out of shape, and would have had trouble convincing a child that he was a common laborer. Within a mile of crossing Boston Neck, Smith was gasping for breath and hungry and the two men were soon seated inside Brewster's tavern for a meal. The same waitress who had identified the British officers several weeks earlier quickly spotted the hard-to-miss Colonel Smith and explained as she took his order, "Colonel Smith, you will find employment enough for you and all of Gage's men in a few months." The startled and exhausted Colonel quickly convinced himself that he could not accomplish his mission and he gratefully turned around and headed back to the comforts of Boston after giving Howe a notebook, pencils, letters of introduction and 10 guineas, and assigned him to complete the mission alone.

Corporal Howe defies the stereotype of unimaginative, less-than-intelligent British enlisted men of the 18th century. The young corporal almost immediately changed his cover to that of a journeyman gunsmith and within hours of his arrival in Concord he was repairing patriots' muskets, dining with the town's militia officers and obtaining intelligence from Major John Buttrick, one of the senior militia commanders. The patriots seemed eager to impress Howe with their firepower and eagerly showed him most of the major supply depots. After scoring this intelligence bonanza, the young corporal casually informed the militia leaders that he could repair far more of their weapons if he could return to his home in Pownall Borough for his tools. The officers agreed and urged him to hurry back with his equipment. At 2 A.M. on April 14, Howe rode back into Boston and was rushed immediately to Gage's headquarters with his detailed information. Gage was already seated at a conference table meeting with his senior officers when Howe entered the room, and in a scene that must have been shocking to a British enlisted man, Gage rose and embraced the young corporal, asked him to sit down with the officers and recount his adventures. Gage asked his frank opinion of the possibility of a successful march to Worcester to destroy the stores there. Howe replied that such an expedition over nearly 50 miles of winding roads, hampered with a necessary train of artillery, could result in a military disaster, especially on the return route. Gage then brought up the possibility of Concord as a target and the corporal was slightly more optimistic, although he warned his commander that the Regulars could expect little help from the largely terrorized Loyalists and that a mounted raid had a much higher probability of success than an infantry expedition. While the British commander felt that he didn't have enough horses to initiate a full-scale cavalry strike, he essentially accepted the advice of this intrepid corporal and designated the town of Concord as the first target in a war that was now clearly imminent.

The Colonial Forces on the Eve of War

While the colonial militia were derided by many British leaders as a "rabble in arms," the men who would face the redcoats in battle were generally well adapted to fighting in the American countryside. Much of the British criticism of colonial units stemmed from their informal appearance and lack of attention to parade ground drill, but most provincial officers consciously ignored close order drill in favor of more realistic training in marksmanship and bush fighting, key elements of the style of warfare that would begin with the Boston campaign.

The nature of community supported militia units meant that at the opening of hostilities the basic colonial organizational unit would be the company, not the regiment. Each colony operated a militia system that listed regiments and even occasional brigades in its tables of organization, but the decentralization of an agricultural society meant that full-fledged regimental exercises were extremely rare in peacetime. Massachusetts developed its regiments by county affiliation and could theoretically field 45 regiments in a full militia mobilization, a force about two-thirds the size of the entire infantry roll of the British army. However, supply problems and the necessity of most men to work continuously on their farms meant that the entire provincial army would almost never be placed in the field at the same time and place.

The social gulf between American militia officers and enlisted men was small compared to British counterparts, but the election of officers was generally not as frivolous or shallow as critics insisted. A significant percentage of the officers elected were chosen by their neighbors because of their experience in serving in provincial units during the wars against the French and Indians and/or because they demonstrated leadership qualities in their relationships within the community. In many respects this was a more logical selection process than the British system in which the oldest sons of wealthy families inherited the father's property while younger sons were packed off to the army by accident of birth.

At the outbreak of the war, colonial militia units were both well-trained and well-equipped to fight a fast moving, mobile conflict using the geography and terrain of America to maximum advantage. On the other hand, the provincials were not particularly well prepared to engage the British Regulars on an open field containing little or no cover. Not only were the rebels relatively untrained for this sort of fighting, they were also very short of men equipped with muskets that could carry a bayonet, the key offensive weapon employed by the British. During the Boston campaign and subsequent engagements such as Long Island, Brandywine, Paoli and Camden, American militiamen caught on the same open ground as bayonet-wielding British Regulars were fortunate to escape annihilation. On the other hand, as demonstrated during the British retreat from Concord, the first two assaults on Breed's Hill and the action around Dorchester Heights, when the colonials could employ the advantage of either natural or man-made cover, the regulars would be in serious trouble.

The men who served in colonial militia units were much more representative of the mainstream of American society than the redcoats were of British society. Most colonies obliged the majority of males between 16 and 60 to enroll in militia units with some exemptions granted to clergymen, college students, physicians and a few other categories. Thus each province could theoretically enlist virtually all of the active males in the colony to serve in the military for relatively brief periods of time. The major limitations on the size of colonial militia forces were not the availability of manpower, but chronic shortages of gunpowder, supply wagons, clothing and, above all, the need to employ most males in the colony in the demanding tasks of an agricultural society. The result was a constant turnover in most units where men would serve in the army for a short period, return home to tend the crops and then return to soldiering. Thus while British generals had a fairly good idea of how many men they could put in the field for a particular campaign, American commanders would watch their armies expand and contract dramatically. During the Boston campaign the colonial army fluctuated between fewer than 6,000 men and more than 20,000 men depending on the day on which unit strengths were tallied.

Arms, Dress and Equipment of Colonial Militiamen

The men who served in colonial militia units were armed and clothed primarily to operate effectively in the highly variable climate and extremely wooded countryside of 18th-century New England. A few elite Massachusetts companies dressed in the blue coats and red trimming popularized by the colony's provincial regiments during the French and Indian War, but most companies mustered men who simply wore everyday clothes to battle. While men from Boston militia units would sometimes wear the famous tricorn hats of the era, most patriot soldiers wore floppy, wide-brimmed hats that were essential to virtually every New England farmer who faced torrential rain, snow and torrid sunlight in his fields. A few officers and a small number of enlisted men wore their old blue provincial army coats, but most men wore either linen dusters or heavier coats that used green or brown dyes derived from local trees. The more famous blue and buff uniform worn by George Washington and later adopted by most Continental Line regiments was actually the Virginia provincial uniform during the French and Indian War and had never been seen in Massachusetts before the arrival of the new commander in chief in June of 1775.

A significant number of militiamen believed that coats were too cumbersome to wear marching or in battle and these troops usually wore what were popularly called "hunting shirts," which were either linen or a combination of linen and wool. These shirts were made long enough to hang just above the knees and were worn tied at the waist with a large belt that could hold a hatchet, knife and one or two pistols. This shirt was essentially a pullover with no buttons, doubled over from one side to the other. It could be bunched up to form a loose pouch in the front. The 10 companies of riflemen from Pennsylvania and Maryland who served in the Boston campaign wore an offshoot of the hunting shirt called the "rifle shirt" which was frequently of fringed buckskin and quickly identified by British Regulars who watched the "shirtmen" pick off their sentries and officers at astounding distances.

Military historians have carried on a running debate over whether the patriots fought the Boston campaign armed primarily with British-style muskets or frontier-style rifles. Actually, it seems that a middle ground is most likely. Most units designated as minuteman companies were interested in arming at least part of their force with muskets that were capable of carrying a bayonet, the

most effective counter to a British bayonet charge. However, other militiamen preferred to use their personal long-barreled hunting muskets which had a range somewhere between a Brown Bess (the standard British shoulder arm) and a Pennsylvania rifle. At least a few colonials acquired the expensive long rifles from gunsmiths or traders who had brought the weapons north from Pennsylvania or Maryland.

Since relatively few colonial soldiers carried bayonets, they attempted to compensate by arming themselves with a variety of close-in weapons. One technique was to carry some combination of sword, hunting knife and tomahawk to parry bayonet thrusts. Another alternative was to provide short-range firepower without the necessity of reloading frequently. However, even with these precautions a British bayonet assault was the most terrifying element of an engagement with the Regulars and would be avoided whenever possible during the Boston campaign.

The British Army on the Eve of War

The British army that was deployed at the beginning of 1775 was still very much on a peacetime establishment and was considerably overextended for the size of the empire. The Regular army included 39,000 infantrymen deployed in 72 regiments of foot, 7,000 horsemen deployed in 25 regiments of cavalry and dragoons, and 3,000 artillerymen serving in a variety of batteries and battalions. Most of this force was still based in the British Isles,

with 16,000 men serving in England and Scotland and 12,000 more maintaining British rule in Ireland. The rest of the army was scattered in dozens of outposts from Gibraltar to India and not readily available for service in America.

The basic operational unit was the regiment, which in infantry formations was made up of 10 companies theoretically deploying 100 men each. However, during peacetime a British infantry company was fortunate to muster on its rolls even half that number, with a typical unit deploying a captain, two lieutenants, two sergeants, three corporals and around 40 privates. Even this number was inflated by the fact that most companies carried several "phantom" names on the muster roll—fictitious names that were carried on the list to secure extra money for the regimental commander, who was able to pocket the pay of these bogus soldiers.

Eight of the regiment's companies were "battalion" or "centre" companies. Two companies were made up of grenadiers and light infantrymen. During active operations, the grenadier and light companies of several regiments were often stripped away to form composite battalions, as they were at Bunker Hill.

The British army in 1775 was theoretically a volunteer force which used a wide variety of techniques to induce men to accept the king's shilling, the symbol of formal enlistment. The existence of over 200 crimes that could be punished by hanging encouraged an arrangement between judges and recruiting sergeants in which a convicted felon was offered enlistment in the army as an alternative to execution. Dozens of bored country laborers were enticed to enlist to escape poverty and boredom, little realizing that they were signing a virtual lifetime contract at ridiculously low wages. Before the expansion of the crisis in America, enlistment standards included a height of at least five foot six inches, an absence of any ruptures and membership in a Protestant denomination. However, as the size of the army was doubled over the course of the war, standards were reduced to a height of five foot three inches and Roman Catholics, especially from Ireland, were welcomed into the army by the thousands in order to produce a field force of 110,000 men to fight simultaneous wars against America, France and Spain.

While the roll of enlisted men was primarily filled by the dregs of British society, officers' commissions were mainly reserved for the upper or upper-middle classes. Other than rare battlefield commissions, most spots in the officer corps were purchased from someone already holding a rank and either moving up to a higher rank or resigning from the service. Terms of purchase were negotiable, but a fairly standard price for a commission as ensign was about £400, about five times the yearly earnings of an average shop owner, while a lieutenant colonelcy in an elite regiment of foot guards went for around £7,000, about twice the annual salary of a cabinet minister. This enormous purchase price resulted in exceptionally wealthy men buying colonel's commissions for their 20-year-old sons while less fortunate men remained in the rank of lieutenant for 30 or 40 years.

The British army at the outbreak of the American Revolution was an organization that was simultaneously hidebound and innovative. On the one hand, some officers were obsessed with maintaining even ranks on the field, treated their men as little more than two-legged animals, and could only think of battle within the confines of an engagement on an open field with no complicating factors. However, other leaders treated their men quite well, valued the opinions of subordinates, and spent long hours devising plans to improve the mobility of British units. Each tendancy would be substantially represented in both the Boston campaign and the rest of the war, as mindless attacks up fortified hills were interspersed with daring night attacks, employment of rifle units and sharpshooters and audacious amphibious assaults behind the American rear. This army was capable of defeating the patriots if properly employed and properly commanded, but was still relatively ponderous and led by a large proportion of officers who could not appreciate the opportunities and dangers of warfare in the American wilderness.

Arms, Uniforms and Equipment of the British Army

The British Regulars of the last quarter of the 18th century were attired in uniforms that were among the most non-utilitarian of any fighting force in history. Soldiers were expected to march and fight dressed in bizarre offshoots of European high fashion of the time, including tricorn hats that were too small to fit snugly on a soldier's head, powdered hair or wigs meant for balls or banquets, and white stockings that were impossible to keep clean even in non-military circles. While the eight Regular battalion companies of each regiment began the American Revolution wearing the famous three-cornered hats, the elite flank companies were saddled with even less utilitarian headgear. The relatively newly-developed light infantry companies wore tight black leather helmets decorated with feathers or horsehair which offered little protection against wet weather and cracked in extensive sunlight. The century-old grenadier units, who had initially been employed tossing huge, clumsy hand grenades into enemy fortifications, wore tall bearskin caps decorated with metal faceplates and backplates which included regimental affiliation in Roman numerals. Since the grenadier units had already recruited the tallest men available, the addition of mitre-like caps was expected to create a stunning and terrifying visual perception of height among the enemy troops. Unfortunately for the men wearing this headgear, the hats were very top heavy and were difficult to keep in place when running toward the enemy lines. The restricted mobility caused by the somewhat ludicrous hats worn by both battalion and flank companies was heightened by the addition of black leather stocks worn at the neck and designed to keep the soldier's chin facing upwards. This device tended to reduce peripheral vision and impede soldiers' ability to shift the direction of their fire rapidly.

The focal point of a British Regular's uniform was the famous red coat. Since enlisted men were issued coats made of cheaper grades of wool and cheaper dyes, their uniforms were usually a faded brick color while only sergeants and officers wore the bright scarlet outfits that would become legendary in paintings and other illustrations. The rest of the enlisted man's uniform included a coarse white shirt, a white waistcoat and white breeches that were worn with stockings in summer and gaiters in winter. Light infantrymen, who were expected to be more mobile, wore tight-fitting red jackets instead of full-length coats, while all enlisted men were issued white or gray overcoats for winter wear in Canadian encampments.

Contrary to much popular literature about the British army in the Revolution, a significant number of regimental commanders experimented with more practical uniforms as the war dragged on. Several regiments abandoned tricorn hats in favor of modified wide-brimmed hats somewhat like the headgear worn by the patriots during the Boston campaign. A number of regimental commanders adopted short jackets for all of their men and replaced stockings, gaiters and breeches with long trousers or coveralls which were far more practical in the wilderness. Some officers ordered their men to dispose of their leather stocks in order to provide more mobility and a few even allowed troops to march and fight without their red coats in particularly hot weather.

The variety caused by these variations within the Regular units was accentuated when Loyalist and German units were deployed. Tory regiments were outfitted in a variety of uniforms ranging from regulation red coats to coats of "Tory green" to civilian clothing that was essentially undistinguishable from many patriot troops. The German mercenaries, who included Hessians, Brunswickers and units from a number of smaller principalities, generally wore mitre caps and long blue coats whose facings varied in color by individual regiment.

The weapon carried by most mainstream British infantry regiments was the famous Brown Bess musket which was a 4-foot-10-inch long weapon weighing 15 pounds and designed to carry a 14-inch socket bayonet with a three-sided blade. The effective range of this weapon was about 70 yards and thus British tactics were based on concentration of firepower and speed of reloading rather than accuracy or marksmanship. As the war progressed, some special units of Regulars and a number of Tory contingents began using longer range rifles to counteract the relatively numerous patriot rifle companies. A few men were even armed with Major Patrick Ferguson's revolutionary breech-loading rifle, which might have changed the nature of the war if it had ever been produced in quantity. Officers almost always carried a sword and occasionally armed themselves with either a pistol or short-barreled musket but these weapons were not always officially authorized and firearms seem to have been seldom carried by field grade officers. Among mounted units, Regular cavalrymen relied primarily on cavalry sabres supplemented by long-barreled horse pistols carried in holsters mounted on the side of the saddle. On the other hand dragoons, while mounted troops, fought primarily on foot and depended on short-barreled muskets supplemented by short-barreled pistols carried by officers.

CHAPTER II

Confrontation on
Lexington Green

On the afternoon of April 14, 1775, His Majesty's dispatch ship *Nautilus* arrived in Boston Harbor and disembarked its most important passenger, Captain Oliver De Lancey of the 17th Light Dragoons. The 21-year-old cavalryman was the American born nephew of the royal governor of New York, the nephew of General Gage's wife and a member of one of the richest families in the colonies. The young Eton graduate had been sent by Lord Dartmouth to deliver a vital memorandum to the commander of British forces in America. The British minister informed Gage that his request for 20,000 reinforcements had been partially approved with the addition of an extra cavalry regiment, three infantry regiments and another detachment of Royal Marines to supplement already promised reinforcements. Dartmouth suggested that any remaining shortfall of men could be made up by raising a corps of volunteers among the loyal subjects of Massachusetts who could be armed with surplus British weapons. The dispatch from the Secretary of State for North America also virtually ordered his military commander to initiate hostilities against colonial rebels as "the Kings's dignity and the honor and safety of the Empire require that, in such a situation, force should be repelled with force." Dartmouth insisted, "it is the opinion of the king's servants, in which His Majesty concurs, that the first essential step towards re-establishing government would be to arrest or imprison the principal actors and abettors of the Provincial Congress whose proceedings appear in every light to be acts of treason and rebellion." The cabinet minister hoped that Gage would make effective use of the reinforcements that would reach him later in the spring, but he also insisted that the general should not wait for these additional troops to open the campaign as "the people, unprepared to encounter with a regular force, cannot be formidable, and though such a proceeding should be, according to your idea of it, a signal for hostilities, yet it will surely be better that the conflict be brought on, upon such ground, than in a riper state of rebellion."

Gage was willing to implement his superiors' orders to initiate offensive operations against the provincials, but he had no intention of following Dartmouth's instructions to begin hostilities by arresting patriot leaders such as Samuel Adams and John Hancock. The general decided instead to buy time

Samuel Adams

John Hancock

until negotiations between the ministry and the colonials were opened or the promised reinforcements arrived. Gage believed that the best way to buy this time was to capture the rebel military stores at Concord, followed by a possible similar strike at Worcester if all went well in the first expedition. The British commander was reasonably confident that an elite strike force could seize or destroy an enormous quantity of colonial munitions and be back in Boston before the provincials fully understood what had occurred.

The general's basic plan of operation was to send a detachment of 10 companies of light infantry, 10 companies of grenadiers and a company of Royal Marines on a nighttime forced march to Concord where the redcoats could enter the town at dawn, capture or destroy the huge cache of rebel supplies and return to Boston before the colonists could fully mobilize their militia units. Gage's plan was actually fairly daring for such a normally conservative officer, but the success of the raid would depend on excellent coordination of disparate units and the presence of an energetic field commander, neither of which would ultimately emerge.

Once Gage had finalized his plan, he met with his naval counterpart, Admiral Samuel Graves, to discuss the maritime aspects of the operation. Gage and Graves despised one another, but while the general was at least reasonably honest and intelligent, the senior admiral in America was a petulant, corrupt and stupid man who owed his command entirely to cronyism in the Admiralty office. Graves agreed to Gage's request for the loan of 20 ships' longboats to be used in ferrying the redcoats from Boston to the mainland, but he also ordered all the designated craft to be moored under the sterns of the warships while they were re-fitted and painted, an operation that was so noticeable that within 24 hours half the population of Boston was speculating about the possibility of a British raid.

On Tuesday, April 18, final preparations for the march to Concord were initiated. Gage sent out a mounted patrol of 10 officers and 10 sergeants under Major Edward Mitchell with orders to intercept any suspected colonial messenger seen riding between Charlestown and Concord. These specially selected men cantered out into the Massachusetts countryside with pistols and swords bulging under their overcoats and their very presence started an alarm around the nearby towns as patriot officers quickly suspected that these heavily-armed men were not out for a recreational ride. When the mounted Regulars began questioning travelers about the whereabouts of Sam Adams and John Hancock, colonial riders hurried to the Reverend Jonas Clarke's home in Lexington to warn his two famous guests that the British might be planning a raid to arrest them. One of the town's leading patriots, Sergeant William Munroe, hurriedly dispatched a squad of militiamen to the Clarke house and ordered the men to defend Adams and Hancock if the redcoats suddenly appeared.

While most prominent patriots in Boston had abandoned the city during the past winter, Dr. Joseph Warren, an influential member of the Provincial Congress and the Committee of Safety, had purposely remained behind to secure more information about Gage's strength and intentions. Warren had set up an effective intelligence system using tavern keepers, wait-

Clarke's house at Lexington, where Samuel Adams and John Hancock were staying on the morning of April 19, 1775.

resses, stableboys and other workers who had regular contact with the British troops to gain valuable information about possible redcoat operations that were under consideration. Shortly after Gage finalized the Concord expedition plans, an unknown messenger delivered an extensive summary of the operation to Warren's house. Since Gage later acknowledged that only his senior subordinate, General Hugh Percy, and Gage's own wife, Margaret, enjoyed initial access to the entire plan, it seems quite probable that Margaret Kemble Gage was, in fact, a rebel sympathizer, a supposition supported by the fact that after the battle Gage sent his wife into virtual exile in England and abandoned her upon his own return later that year.

As soon as Warren received this vital information, he contacted one of the most reliable patriot couriers, Paul Revere, to help coordinate the alarm system throughout the countryside. William Dawes, a Boston tanner who had established good relations with British sentries at key checkpoints, was chosen to slip past the redcoat guards to deliver a warning to

Paul Revere later in life. An engraving based on a portrait by Gilbert Stuart.

Hancock and Sam Adams, and then ride to Concord with the information that "a large body of the king's troops, supposed to be a brigade of 12 or 1,500, are embarked in boats for Boston and have gone to land at Lechmere's Point." Meanwhile, Revere was asked to take an identical message to Lexington and Concord by an alternate route that would include a water passage to Charlestown and an overland ride between Charlestown and Lexington. Revere immediately contacted Captain John Pulling, vestryman of Christ Church, and Robert Newman, sexton of the building which was popularly called Old North Church. Newman's invalid mother used her home as a boarding house for British officers, and when Revere rushed up to the front door, he stopped just in time to observe a parlor full of redcoats smoking and playing cards. The silversmith went to the back of the house, slipped through a gate into the garden and almost collided with the sexton who had just crawled out of an upstairs window and dropped to the ground. The two men collected the waiting vestryman and hurried over to the church where they climbed more than 150 creaking steps to the church tower; then climbed even higher on a narrow ladder which reached the topmost window in the steeple.

On the other side of the Charles River, Charlestown patriots had been alerted to watch for a signal from Old North which would provide information concerning the march route of the redcoats. One lantern would be a signal that the Regulars were taking the more roundabout land route; two lanterns would notify the men that the British were coming across the river. Now that Warren had informed Revere of the redcoats' plans, the courier held two lanterns out of the northwest corner window of the Old North steeple. The Charlestown men saw two dim yellow lights flicker for a moment or two and then Revere and his associates extinguished the candles and cleared out of the church, barely avoiding a British patrol a few hundred feet down the street. Revere then made his way to the waterfront and climbed clumsily into a small boat that he had hidden for just such an emergency. Two experienced sailors were available to help him cross to Charlestown and the three men pushed off into Boston Harbor. As the small vessel was rowed across the harbor, the patriots came dangerously close to the British warship *Somerset* floating menacingly above them. The Americans could easily hear the ship's bells strike five times, which meant it was 10:30 P.M., and could clearly see armed sentries posted fore and aft. However, despite the presence of a brilliant near-full moon, the warship's 64 guns remained silent as the small boat moved quietly toward the Charlestown ferry landing. The two oarsmen wished Revere Godspeed and the courier stepped ashore to begin his famous ride.

While Revere was being rowed across the Charles River, Colonel William Conant of the Charlestown militia was preparing to expedite the courier's mission. Conant asked Deacon John Larkin, a wealthy local merchant, to loan Revere his fast, dependable horse and had the mount fully outfitted when the Boston silversmith arrived. Soon after Revere thanked his fellow patriots and rode off into the countryside, his mission almost came to an end. Two of the mounted officers that Gage had posted along the road caught sight of the courier and attempted to cut him off. Revere had a faster and more maneuverable horse which allowed him to ride cross-country, which left the roadbound officers increasingly far behind. The courier then rode through the town of Menotomy, present day Arlington, turned onto the King's Highway, and headed toward Lexington as he warned local residents along the way "that the Regulars are coming out."

A reasonable representation of Paul Revere on his ride. Revere's riding boots and saddlery are accurate, but most militiamen were not as well-equipped as this sentry.

When Revere arrived in Lexington, his main task was to warn Hancock and Adams that they might be one of the major targets of the British raid. However, when the courier arrived at the Clarke house, Sgt. Munroe urged him to lower his voice as the noise would wake up the sleeping patriot leaders. Revere brusquely replied "Noise! You'll have noise enough before long! The Regulars are coming out!" Hancock and Adams were still awake and quickly invited Revere inside where the three men reviewed the situation. The patriots were soon joined by William Dawes who had just arrived from an alternate route to Lexington and the two couriers agreed to adjourn to nearby Buckman's Tavern while Hancock and Adams decided their course of action. The two riders were met at the tavern by the commander of the local militia company, Captain John Parker, who used the couriers' news to order a mobilization of his men on the field outside the tavern. Thus at about 1 A.M. on Wednesday, April 19, 1775, several dozen sleepy, bewildered militiamen straggled into a darkened field to await a possible attack from soldiers who were still very much their own countrymen.

While Parker's men began deploying near Buckman's Tavern, Gage's intricate timetable for the expedition was already beginning to unravel. At nine o'clock Tuesday night, almost 800 British soldiers were awakened and told to dress quietly, pick up provisions and draw 36 rounds of powder and ball. The soldiers were conducted out of the back entrance of the barracks buildings and ordered to move in small parties through the largely deserted streets while a security detachment ensured secrecy by bayoneting any dog that began to bark and detaining any civilian who strayed too close to the gathering redcoats. The sleepy and confused Regulars were ordered to report to an empty beach at the edge of Back Bay, and over the next hour companies of light infantry and grenadiers slowly drifted in from Boston Common, Fort Hill and the North End. Finally, at ten o'clock that evening, Lt. Colonel Francis Smith arrived to take charge of 21 companies of Regulars and a small party of Loyalist volunteers who would serve as scouts and guides. Smith's rapid abandonment of the earlier scouting mission assigned to him by Gage seems to have done little to diminish his commander's opinion of his talents and this slow, ponderous, overweight officer now showed up late for the first campaign of the war. The late arriving colonel was almost immediately faced with a crisis as Admiral Graves had provided only enough ships' boats to ferry 400 men in one crossing. Company commanders largely ignored Smith's presence as they vied to embark their men in one of the limited number of vessels. For example, the aggressive adjutant of the 23rd Regiment of Foot, Lt. Frederick Mackenzie, quickly commandeered enough boats to hold his regiment's light infantry and grenadier companies and simply ordered the sailors to shove off before Smith fully comprehended what was happening.

After the small boats had ferried about 400 men across the Charles River, the vessels returned to a scene of continuing confusion as junior officers attempted to bully young naval midshipmen into taking their company before others, while Smith did little to restore order to the proceedings. One of the most sophisticated observers of the embarkation, Ensign Jeremy Lister of the 10th Regiment of Foot, had only come down to the beach to wish good luck to several of his comrades who served in light infantry or grenadier companies. However, when a lieutenant of the 10th's light infantry company sent a questionable message from his quarters that he was too sick to take part in the operation, Lister quickly volunteered to take his place and jumped in a boat just as it pushed off into the river.

The embarkation and transfer of the second wave of redcoats consumed another hour of valuable darkness and it was past midnight before Smith climbed out of the final boat and formed his men at Lechmere Point. The force was then ordered to move forward through a series of waist-deep swamps and inlets which thoroughly soaked the men and slowed the march to a crawl. However, after marching just far enough to become thoroughly soaked, the men were ordered to halt; Smith suddenly realized that the navy had promised to furnish rations for the expedition. Ironically, each company commander had already issued his men with enough army rations for a one-day march, but Smith insisted on waiting for the "official" naval supplies to be ferried over from Boston. Two hours later a string of naval craft landed and sailors began unloading boxes of "ship's biscuits" which were crawling with so many maggots that they looked inedible even in the darkness. Each redcoat was duly issued his "official" ration for the march which in most cases he promptly threw by the roadside, sneering at the level of food his naval counterparts were forced to consume. After the British Regulars had been shivering on the road for this two-hour delay they were ordered forward into a new series of swamps which thoroughly soaked the men again before they reached slightly firmer ground.

Smith was still not finished with his attempts to lose all possibility of surprise on the march to Concord. The ponderous colonel, ever attuned to His Majesty's regulations, now decided that it would be improper to conduct a march in a random order of companies and ordered another halt while the entire force was deployed. As the stoic redcoats stood shivering on an oozing, muddy roadside, the whole column was arranged in a new order in which lowest-numbered, most senior units were placed in the front while higher-numbered junior elements brought up the rear. Finally, after almost another hour of shouted commands and rearrangement of lines, Smith was ready to give the order to march inland. Since less than two hours of darkness still remained when the first company actually headed for Concord, the whole concept of a dawn raid on the town had now disintegrated. The redcoats would now face an increasingly aroused countryside and would be fortunate to reach Lexington before dawn.

The British expedition commander had managed to completely bungle the first stage of an intricately planned operation but he now expected his men to regain much of the time that he had lost. Smith treated his soldiers as little more than two-legged animals and now he amplified his lack of concern by ordering the column into a murderously swift double-quick march. Shivering, fatigued and still soaked men were

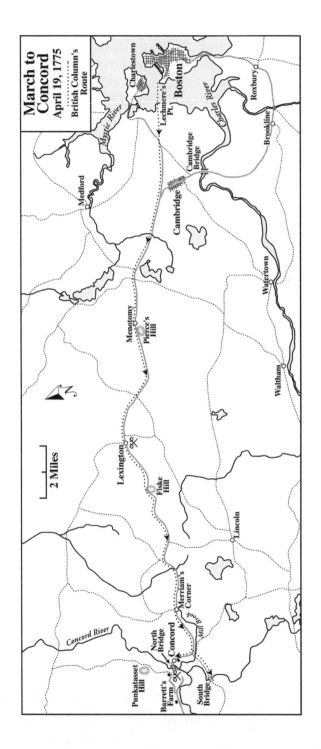

March to Concord
April 19, 1775
British Column's Route

Charlestown

Boston

Lechmere's Pt.

Charles River

Roxbury

Brookline

Cambridge Bridge

Mystic River

Medford

Cambridge

Watertown

Menotomy

Pierce's Hill

Waltham

2 Miles

Lexington

Fiske Hill

Lincoln

Merriam's Corner

Mill Brook

Concord River

North Bridge

Concord

Punkatasset Hill

Barrett's Farm

South Bridge

now ordered to increase their speed to over five miles an hour while carrying over 100 pounds of equipment and constricted by perhaps the most non-functional uniforms in military history. The panting Regulars finally entered the "Great Road" that led to Lexington and then Concord and flank units began picking up unsuspecting colonists who were unfortunate enough to be abroad that April night. When some of the prisoners bragged that the local militia units were already aware of the presence of the redcoats, the increasingly agitated Smith ordered his second in command, Royal Marine Major John Pitcairn, to take six companies of the slightly less encumbered light infantry and quick-march to Concord to secure the town's two bridges before the provincials either occupied them or destroyed them.

While the redcoats endured their on-again, off-again march inland, the village of Lexington was a focal point of provincial activity. Samuel Adams spent much of the night attempting to convince John Hancock that he was badly needed in the Provincial Congress and should abandon his idea to grab a musket and fight alongside the Lexington militia when the Regulars arrived. As Adams and Hancock argued, Paul Revere and William Dawes prepared their horses for a dash

An early 19th-century map of Lexington and Concord. Town center is (3), the militia assembled behind hill (6). Road and bridge (10) were built in 1793, roads and bridges marked (5), (7), (8), and (11) were in use in 1775.

to Concord to complete their night's work. As they were preparing to saddle up, they were joined by a young Concord physician, Dr. Samuel Prescott, who had spent the evening with his fiancée, Lydia Milliken, and was just leaving Lexington when he encountered the couriers. Prescott, who considered himself a "high patriot," quickly convinced the two men that his knowledge of the local countryside could expedite their mission and they readily agreed to his company. However, less than a mile outside of Lexington the men were surrounded by four mounted British officers who yelled "stop, if you go an inch further, you are dead men." As the patriot riders were herded into a nearby pasture, Prescott whispered to Revere to make a break and the two men galloped toward a low stone wall followed closely by the British riders. The Concord physician's horse cleared the fence and Prescott disappeared into the woods to alert the residents of his community. However, Revere's horse could not make the jump and the silversmith was quickly surrounded by redcoats including two men who had been guarding Dawes. The Boston tanner used this brief diversion to spur his own horse into a nearby field, although a few minutes later the mount threw him off, forcing the courier to limp painfully back into Lexington.

Two patriot couriers had escaped the British trap, but the redcoats could still grill their one remaining prisoner. When a British officer politely addressed the well-dressed silversmith asking "may I crave your name, sir?" the redcoats were pleasantly surprised to discover they had bagged one of the most famous patriot leaders. A few minutes later, when the scouting party's commander, Major Edward Mitchell, cantered up to the group of horsemen, civility quickly vanished. The British major pointed a pistol at Revere's head and told him he would blow out his brains if he failed to respond truthfully to a series of questions. The patriot "express" rider calmly told the grim major the "truth" that he had personally observed over 500 militiamen deploying around Buckman's Tavern and that thousands of additional provincials were at this moment closing in on Smith's column from the rear. Mitchell was appalled at this startling news and after commandeering Revere's horse, set the courier free while he spurred back down the road to warn Smith of a possible rebel ambush.

While Revere walked back toward Lexington, Captain Parker was attempting to decide the next course of action for his Lexington militiamen. When no news of the British advance reached the village after the deployment at Buckman's Tavern, Parker allowed his men to return home pending the completion of a scouting mission that he had assigned to four riders. At least three of the scouts were captured by Mitchell's screening party but the fourth man made his way back to Lexington a little before dawn with word that the redcoats were about a half hour behind him. When Parker originally called out the Lexington militia company, almost the whole force of 130 men had responded. However, many of the men had now drifted back to homes some distance away, and when the captain recalled his unit, only 70 or 80 colonists gathered around the tavern. Ironically, these men were not the fabled minutemen of legend since the town of Lexington had largely ignored the Provincial Congress' mandate to divide eligible men into militia, alarm and minuteman companies. Parker and his fellow town leaders had elected to maintain a single, very large company that included virtually every able bodied male between 16 and 70. Almost a third of this force was related to either Parker or his wife and the 46-year-old veteran of Rogers' Rangers was viewed as the most logical man to command this unit. However, Parker was also dying of consumption and would be dead before the end of the year, a grim reality that was dramatically displayed in the captain's hollow cheeks and fever-tinged eyes. Parker knew that his seven children would soon be orphans whether or not he survived a now-imminent encounter with the approaching Regulars.

Parker subsequently deployed the 70 or 80 men who had responded to his second summons along the upper right-hand corner of the town common in a double file to partially disguise the small size of the force. Meanwhile, Major Pitcairn was hurrying toward Lexington with his advance unit of six companies of light infantry. The 50-year-old Marine had already boasted about his ability to march roughshod through the American "peasants" with only a few companies of Royal Marines, saying "If I draw my sword halfway out of my scabbard, they will all quickly run away." Pitcairn's men were approaching Lexington just before dawn on this epic Wednesday morning and in the half light of the almost breaking day, the major thought he saw as many as 300 provincials lined along the village green, a force that seemed to outnumber his own detachment of about 250 redcoats.

As the Regulars approached Lexington, they were confronted by a fork in the road which divided the main route to Concord on the left from a spur of the Bedford road on the right. The ground between the two roads essentially formed the apex of an inverted triangle that marked the town's common with the Lexington militia deployed in a position that would in no way hinder the British march to Concord.

When the British detachment approached to within a few hundred yards of the Lexington village green, Pitcairn halted his men, ordered them to load their muskets with powder and ball, and then resumed the advance toward the fork in the road which featured the town's meetinghouse at the point of intersection and Buckman's Tavern 100 feet away just on the other side of the Bedford road. For reasons that are still not clear to this day, the final approach of the British advance party to Lexington became very spread out so that command of the two most forward companies fell to young lieutenant Jesse Adair while Pitcairn rode to the back of the column to hurry the remaining men forward. As Adair approached the fork in the road he could see that the road to Concord was unobstructed, but he also noticed Parker's company deployed near the Bedford road on the far side of the common, about a hundred yards beyond the meetinghouse. While the provincials were making no attempt to interfere with the British advance, Adair became convinced that marching up a road with a band of armed rebels hovering on his right flank, even if at a distance, was an intolerable breach of security, and he ordered his men to march across the common and then deploy into a line of battle perhaps 50 yards from the militiamen.

Thus at this critical moment, Pitcairn had lost touch with his most advanced units and a young lieutenant was unilaterally creating a confrontation with the colonists. The two companies, the light infantry of the 4th and 10th regiments, formed a long red line as sergeants and junior officers dropped back to take their proper combat positions. The Regulars began shouting their often terrifying "huzzas" and the cheers deafened the shouts of officers. Fifty yards away, the two lines of militiamen were becoming confused and alarmed. When the advancing redcoat column had first been sighted, Parker assured his men that their deployment was mostly symbolic as he ordered "let the troops pass by; don't molest them, without they being first." On the other hand, he had followed this command with a sobering promise that "the first man who offers to run shall be shot down." Now it was obvious that the redcoats were more than willing to provoke a confrontation and Parker and his men estimated that more than a thousand British Regulars were either on the village green or rapidly approaching the meetinghouse, making an exchange of fire almost certain suicide.

When Major Pitcairn heard the loud cheering of his advance detachment, he quickly rode up to the village common and tried to at least partially defuse the confrontation. He ordered his own men to stand fast, but yelled to the colonials to "lay down your arms, you damned rebels! You villains, disperse, damn you, disperse." As this order was shouted, Parker initially ordered his men to remain in place as he yelled "stand your ground, don't fire unless fired upon. But if they want to have a war, let it begin here." Dozens of spectators now lined the periphery of the village green and they began to shudder when many of the redcoats brandished their bayonets in preparation for a charge. As the redcoats began an even louder round of "huzzas," Parker's confidence began to fade and he ordered his men to disperse. However, as the men filed off the green, there was no attempt to lay down their arms as Pitcairn had ordered, and the Marine major now escalated the confrontation by ordering his men to surround the militiamen and forcibly disarm them. However, before this order could even begin to

An early John W. Barber woodcut of the action at Lexington. In contrast to more fanciful later renderings, the buildings are accurate and the British are doing all the shooting.

be implemented, a shot rang out and confrontation turned into bloodshed.

As Parker's men turned away and began to disperse, redcoats, colonials and spectators all heard the sound of a firing weapon but no one could later agree on the direction from which it came. However, what is certain is that this single shot prompted first a few ragged shots from the redcoats and then a full scale volley that ripped through the departing militiamen, many of whom now had their backs turned to the British. For a brief moment, many of the provincials were convinced that the Regulars were not using bullets but were merely attempting to frighten the Americans. However, seconds later, the first colonists began to drop to the ground and the gravity of the situation became increasingly clear. Parker urged his men to get off the field quickly, but as the militiamen withdrew from the common the redcoats lowered their bayonets and prepared to charge. Already several Americans were dead or dying. Samuel Hadley and John Brown were shot in the back on the edge of the common; Asahel Porter, a Woburn man who had been captured by the British patrols, sprinted for his freedom and went down riddled with bullets; Jonathan Harrington made a dash for his nearby home and was mortally wounded just before he reached his doorstep. Now the redcoats lunged at the colonists with bayonets and more Americans went down. Robert Munroe was just aiming his musket when he was stabbed by a bayonet-wielding Regular; Jonas Parker, the militia captain's cousin, had declared he would never run from the redcoats and he calmly placed his musket balls and flints in his hat on the ground and prepared to pick off the advancing British troops; as he was loading his gun he was run through with a British bayonet.

As the redcoats sprinted across the town common, officers almost totally lost control. Pitcairn admitted later "without any order or regularity, the light infantry began a scattering fire" while Lt. John Barker's testimony was more explicit as he in-

The most contemporary, and believed to be the most accurate, depiction of the action at Lexington. Drawn by Ralph Earle and engraved by Amos Doolittle, the British are shown firing on colonists who are dispersing, but who have not laid down their arms as ordered. Major Pitcairn is mounted at right.

sisted, "our men without any orders rushed in upon them (the Americans), fired, and put them to flight." Another officer noted, "firing was continued by our troops as long as any of the provincials were to be seen." While most of the redcoats charged the militiamen on the village green, a detachment of Regulars swarmed around the Lexington meetinghouse. Four colonials had been posted to guard the town's powder supply but when a large number of soldiers closed in on the building, the men attempted to flee. Caleb Harrington was killed near the meetinghouse door and Joseph Comec was wounded a few seconds later. One of the remaining defenders, Joshua Simonds, ducked back into the building and thrust his musket into a powder barrel, ready to explode the whole magazine if the redcoats entered the meetinghouse.

At this point in the action, with over a dozen provincials sprawled in the grass dead or wounded and the redcoats starting to threaten the houses adjoining the common, Colonel Smith arrived on the scene and quickly realized his men were out of control. The colonel rode up to a junior officer, Lieuten-

A fanciful picture of Lexington, but accurate enough for the tactics used by the colonists to harass the British retreat to Boston.

ant Sutherland, and asked "do you know where a drummer is?" A drummer was located and ordered to beat to arms. Slowly, the now rampaging redcoats reluctantly began to pull back from the meetinghouse, the tavern and the private dwellings and drift back to the center of the village green. The troops seemed anything but eager to return to formation. One officer admitted later, "we then formed on the Common, but the men were so wild they could hear no orders." Another officer noted "we formed them on the Common but with some difficulty." Quite simply, the officers of one of the most highly disciplined armies in the world had lost control of their men at a critical point in British-colonial relations and only the intervention of the normally bungling Smith prevented a virtual massacre of Lexington's residents. Smith himself admitted somewhat cryptically, "I was desirous of putting a stop to all further slaughter of those deluded people." Smith had prevented further killing but seven colonists, still British subjects, were lying dead around the town common, while nine more men were wounded, most of them severely. Almost a quarter of the men who had deployed on the village green earlier that morning had been killed or injured while the British column had suffered only one minor casualty in the engagement. The British officers were still barely able to hold their men in check and they were appalled when their commander finally explained the full purpose of their mission. A few officers were bold enough to suggest that it would be suicidal to march even deeper into hostile countryside with "the certainty that the country will be alarmed and assembled" and urged a speedy return to Boston before a disaster occurred. Smith politely ignored their protests and instead focused his attention on his barely controllable enlisted men. Before ordering these men to resume their march he allowed them to fire a victory salute and give three cheers for their triumph. However, as the redcoat column began its march to Concord, eyewitnesses to the engagement were already spreading the alarm across the Massachusetts countryside while the survivors of the Lexington militia mustered again and planned their own form of retribution on the "bloody backs."

Major John Pitcairn and Captain John Parker

The two senior officers of the opposing forces on Lexington Common were both middle-aged men who were very near the end of their lives. Major John Pitcairn, who commanded the advance force of the British column was a 53-year-old Royal Marine officer who commanded the 1st Marine Battalion in Gage's army. His men were the toughest, best-trained men in the Boston garrison and, largely because of Pitcairn, had the best morale. The major was considered to be a strict disciplinarian, but was also noted for his fairness, integrity, and concern for the welfare of his men. On a number of occasions Gage employed Pitcairn to judge disputes that arose between Boston civilians and the British Regulars, and even patriot leaders applauded his concern with justice.

Pitcairn had no particular dislike of Americans and even tolerated the strong patriot sentiments of the son of the owner of the house in which he and his staff resided. However, he consistently downplayed the military capabilities of the colonists, insisting, "these deluded people believe they are invincible.... when this army is ordered to act against them they will soon be convinced they are very insignificant when opposed to regular troops; I am satisfied that one active campaign, a smart action and burning two or three of their towns will set everything to rights." After playing a major role in the actions at Lexington and Concord, Pitcairn led the Marine battalion against the American redoubt at Breed's Hill and was mortally wounded by the black servant of a Connecticut officer just as the redcoats were capturing the position. President Ezra Stiles of Yale College called Pitcairn "a good man in a bad cause."

The American officer who faced Pitcairn on Lexington Green, Captain John Parker, was 46 years old and described by neighbors as "a great tall man with a large head and a high, wide brow." Parker had been an active participant in the colonial wars against the French, having been present at the siege of Louisbourg and the conquest of Quebec and had served in Rogers' Rangers along with a number of other prominent patriot officers. By the fall of 1774 Parker owned a large farm two miles from the center of Lexington village and had been elected as captain of the local militia company which was in the process of being integrated into the "constitutional army" of the province. The Massachusetts provincial congress had authorized him to "make a regular and forcible resistance to any open hostility" of the British Regulars and he had been energetically involved in training his 130-man company in open order skirmishing.

At the time of the British expedition to Concord, Parker was gravely ill with tuberculosis and was described as "gaunt" and "fevered" in appearance. His condition worsened rapidly during the late spring of 1775 and he was unable to command his company during the battle of Bunker Hill. He died on September 17, 1775. His musket was passed on to his grandson, Reverend Theodore Parker, who became a celebrated minister and author and in turn donated the famous weapon to the Massachusetts State House where it became the focal point of public attention for decades.

Paul Revere (1735-1808)

Revere was the son of French Hugue-not immigrant Apollos Rivoire who subsequently anglicized his name and married a local woman named Deborah Hitchbourn. Revere was born December 31, 1735 and attended the North Boston Writing School for five years before becoming an apprentice silversmith at age 13. When Revere was 19, his father died and the son took responsibility for a widowed mother and six younger brothers and sisters. He also became a lieutenant in a Boston artillery company com-manded by future Continental artillerist and engineer Richard Gridley and served with this unit under Lord Loudon against the French at Crown Point.

When Revere returned from the French and Indian War, he opened a silversmith's shop and married Sara Orne, who bore eight children and died in childbirth. The widowed father remarried six months later to Rachel Walker, with whom he had an additional eight children. Revere's political activism began to emerge after the Boston Massacre in March of 1770 when he produced a famous, although inaccurate, engraving of the engagement which was reproduced throughout the colonies. Since Revere was an excellent horseman he fre-quently volunteered for courier assignments that took him to a number of points along the Atlantic coast. He was one of the leaders of the Boston Tea Party activities, and then carried messages of the event into the middle colonies. Revere's horseman-ship, reliability, and ties with Dr.

Joseph Warren led to the assignment to warn the Massachusetts countryside that the regulars were coming out on the eve of Lexington and Concord.

Revere served as both courier and officer during the Boston campaign and was made lieutenant colonel of artillery and commander of Castle William at the time of the British evacuation. This was considered a crucial assignment as it was assumed that the British would attempt to recapture the city in the near future. When the expected attack failed to materialize, Revere secured a state commission as colonel and accompa-nied a Massachusetts militia force in an aborted attempt to capture Rhode Island from the British in 1778. In 1779 Revere was commander of all state artillery forces in the failed Penobscot Bay campaign.

At the end of the Revolution, Revere expanded his silversmith's business to include manufacture of copper sheeting which was used to construct the bottoms of the frigate *Constitution* and other major American warships. His company also manufac-tured the boiler plates for Robert Fulton's newly developed steamships and secured contracts to produce cannons for American forts and warships. When Revere died on May 1,1808, Revere Copper and Brass was one of the country's largest manufac-turing enterprises, while more than 50 grandchildren were alive as potential heirs.

CHAPTER III

Advance and Retreat from Concord

*A*s the British Regulars celebrated their "victory" at Lexington and fell back in formation to resume their march, the now fully alerted militiamen in Concord began preparing for the redcoats' arrival. While Lexington could field only a single company of men, the much larger town of Concord deployed five companies including three Regular militia units, a reserve alarm company and an elite force of minutemen. When word of the British advance reached the town, senior officers from all three services formed a council of war to discuss the most effective approach to meeting the imminent threat. A consensus was finally hammered out in which the younger and more mobile minutemen would screen the Regulars' advance while the remaining four companies would deploy around the town until a definite pattern of action emerged.

The single company of minutemen, just over 70 men strong, marched about a mile east of the town and began to deploy along a prominent ridge. Suddenly, the reality of military opposition to the British empire began to strike home as a column of 21 companies of Regulars was spotted marching down the road less than a mile away. One teenaged minuteman noted "the sun was rising and shined on their arms and they made a noble appearance in their red coats and glistening weapons." Colonel Smith spotted the minutemen at about the same time his own force was detected and the British commander quickly ordered several companies of light infantry to push the provincials off the high ground. The colonials, who were even more mobile and agile than the elite redcoats, calmly waited until the Regulars closed to within 500 yards of the ridge and then scrambled down to the road and began an almost festive march back to town accompanied by the music of several fifers and drummers. A few hundred yards to the east, the main British column held its fire and instead, redcoat bandsmen began playing the same tunes as the colonials as they formed their own procession into Concord, causing at least one of the retreating minutemen to note "we had grand music on our march."

Once the light infantry had secured the high ground approaching Concord, Colonel Smith and Major Pitcairn climbed to a cemetery near the crest of the ridge and pulled out their

In this Earle and Doolittle engraving, Major Pitcairn and Lt. Colonel Francis Smith reconnoiter from Concord's hilltop cemetery as their troops enter the town.

telescopes to study the surrounding countryside. As the two British officers surveyed the terrain, they agreed that speed was becoming critical as "vast numbers of country people were assembling in the distance" and His Majesty's troops might be badly outnumbered before long. Smith ordered the column to enter Concord and then issued orders to his officers. The British commander insisted that company commanders maintain a tight rein on their men to prevent repetition of the bloodbath at Lexington and to insure that no private property was destroyed. No one was to fire unless clearly attacked. Only officers could initiate a search of a building. However, as the redcoats began a systematic search for rebel arms and equipment, Smith began to realize that the "surprise" raid that had been initially conceived by General Gage was not going to accomplish its purpose. While the colonel and his senior officers sat comfortably on borrowed chairs on the front lawns of Concord's best houses, enlisted men and junior officers unearthed a disappointing cache of rebel equipment.

Major Pitcairn and several of his Marines scored the biggest catch of the day when they barged into Ephraim Jones' tavern, put pistols to the innkeeper's head, and forced him to reveal the location of three large 24-pounder cannon buried in the tavern's backyard. The Marine major supervised the spiking of the guns and then treated his men to breakfast, insisting on paying the still quivering Jones a generous amount for the hurriedly prepared meals. However, destruction of the rebel guns represented the only really tangible achievement of the raid, as one of Smith's officers admitted "we did not find so much as we expected," while one British historian was far more blunt, noting sourly, "the grenadiers spoiled some flour, knocked the trunions off several iron guns, burned a heap of wooden spoons and cut down a liberty pole," hardly a satisfying accomplishment for almost one-third of the British army in America. In fact, the almost ritualistic chopping down of Concord's liberty pole, accompanied by the applause of Smith and his senior officers, was the colonel's high point of the day. A systematic search of the town produced only 30 barrels of flour and a cache of lead bullets that were all thrown into a millpond and promptly fished out undamaged the next day.

While Smith and his officers were served breakfast in the comfort of their lawn chairs, the British commander began ordering units to secure the town's two bridges and search possible rebel stores being hidden at Colonel James Barrett's farm two miles outside of town. Three companies under Captain Walter Laurie were ordered to secure North Bridge; a single company under Captain Munday Pole was ordered to march a mile downstream to seize South Bridge; and four companies under Captain Lawrence Parsons were given the task of searching the Barrett farm and destroying anything that might be of use to the provincials.

As the redcoats began their assigned tasks, the provincials began planning their response to the British expedition. Colonel Barrett, who was the senior militia officer in Concord, was delayed arriving in the town while he supervised the removal or hiding of military stores that had been cached on his farm. He and his sons plowed up several fields, planted dozens of muskets in the furrows and covered them up with new earth. Then the colonel hurried toward Concord and assumed command of all available militia forces. The company of minutemen had initially retreated from the ridge containing the town's burying ground to a second position just east of the Concord River called Ripley Hill. But Barrett was convinced that his most valuable company was exposed on the far side of the river and ordered the minutemen to link up with the Regular militia companies on the west side of the river at Punkatasset Hill. The new rallying point was just under a mile from North Bridge and by the time Captain Laurie and his redcoats arrived at that span the British could see hundreds of provincials deploying along the height. By about 9 A.M. elements of two Middlesex regiments had arrived on the scene with units from Acton, Bedford, Lincoln and several other towns to reinforce Barrett's five Concord companies.

At about this time, the now more than 500 provincial troops deployed on Punkatasset Hill detected smoke rising from the center of Concord. Most of the smoke was coming from a British bonfire built to destroy the meager cache of supplies the redcoats had captured. Sparks from the fire had ignited the town's meetinghouse and civilians and redcoats temporarily joined forces to put out the flames. From the distant perspective of the heights, it began to appear that the British fully intended to burn Concord, and Barrett agreed to march down the hill and take up a new position on the town's Regular muster field on a flat hilltop about 1,000 yards closer to the town. The muster field was currently being occupied by two companies of redcoats acting as a screening force for Laurie's bridge guards, but when the Regulars saw hundreds of provincials scrambling down the slopes of Punkatesset and advancing their way, they quickly withdrew toward Laurie's men deployed around the bridge.

When the militiamen reached the drill field, the smoke seemed even more intense in Concord center, and Lt. Joseph Hosmer, an officer in the minuteman company, turned to Barrett and asked "Will you let them burn the town down?" Captain William Smith of the Lincoln militia and Captain Isaac Davis of the Acton contingent immediately supported Hosmer's plea for a general advance and Barrett finally agreed to order the men forward. Barrett formed up the two regiments, ordered the men to load their weapons, and shouted that the troops would not be the first to fire, but if the British did begin shooting, "Fire as fast as you can!" Lt. Colonel John Robinson and Major John Buttrick led the regiments down the hill while a small contingent of fifers and drummers struck up the popular tune "The White Cockade." When Captain Laurie saw his two screening companies withdrawing toward the bridge followed by hundreds of armed colonials he quickly dispatched a messenger to Smith to request reinforcements and ordered his 115 men to fall back to the far side of the river while pulling up the planks on the bridge to delay the colonials if they attempted to charge.

Laurie realized that his three companies were badly outnumbered by the provincials, and his first response to this crisis was to order his men to deploy in a new formation designed for street fighting. This formation deployed the redcoats in columns of fours to maximize their firepower in a small space. Each column would kneel and fire and then break right and left and file to the rear to reload while the next rank in line opened fire to keep successive volleys trained on a larger attacking force. In theory, a narrow alley or bridge could be kept under constant fire, but as one of Laurie's lieutenants noted, "the rebels got so near him his people were obliged to form the best way they could–the three companies got one behind the other so that only the front one could fire." Instead of several crisply formed ranks of Regulars each ready to fire in support of one another, the redcoats were caught in a tangled mass as the two screening companies collided with the rear company and all became intermingled in a mass of milling troops.

Laurie was obviously attempting to form his men to check a colonial advance on North Bridge, but the provincials, although numerous and armed, had not given any evidence that they intended to initiate hostilities against the redcoats. As the advance units of militia began approaching the west side

Militia leader Isaac Davis is killed by a British volley at Concord's North Bridge.

A British company at right fires a volley to cover the British retreat from North Bridge. (Earle and Doolittle)

of the river bank, a shot was fired. Unlike the situation at Lexington a few hours earlier, this time it was clearly a British soldier who fired first, and his shot was followed by two or three others. Then, still without orders, the entire front rank of redcoats discharged a volley. Although most of the bullets sailed over the heads of the advancing colonists, Captain Isaac Davis dropped dead when a bullet pierced his heart; Abner Hosmer, also of Acton, died from a fatal head wound and four other men were wounded. The provincials never broke stride as they advanced to the west end of the bridge, and then Major Buttrick shouted "Fire, fellow soldiers, for God's sake, fire!" The words rang down the ranks and a wall of flame emerged from the front row of militiamen. The first concentrated American volley of the Revolution was far more accurate than its British counterpart and nearly 20 redcoats, including four of Laurie's eight officers, were dead or wounded within a few seconds. As soon as the provincials fired their first volley, they formed into a double firing line that stretched along the causeway that paralleled the Concord River. Additional sheets of flame emerged from the Americans as the Regulars fumbled around attempting to deploy into the ordered street fighting formation. Ensign Jeremy Lister noted "the weight of their fire was such that we were obliged to give way, then run with the greatest precipitance." Laurie's attempt to fully deploy his men simply disintegrated as the redcoat enlisted men ignored the commands of the few surviving officers and started running back toward Concord center.

The retreating British Regulars were now extremely vulnerable to the fire of hundreds of provincials lining the river bank, but the colonial leaders were momentarily stunned by the sight of vaunted professionals running in panic from the despised "country people" and no order to fire was given. Finally, after another impromptu council of war, the various town militia commanders agreed to implement Colonel Barrett's suggestion that all available minutemen companies would cautiously advance over North Bridge and push slowly toward Concord center while the rest of the provincials pulled back to the muster field to await events.

The elite minutemen crossed the river and edged forward through a series of fences and fields, but before they covered even half the distance to the town center, they almost collided with a British relief force commanded by Colonel Smith. The wary colonials fell back a short distance to a small ridge and quickly deployed behind a long, stone wall. In turn, Smith and his reinforcing grenadiers marched up to within 200 yards of the wall and then halted while the colonel and his staff carefully studied the rebel position. Smith accepted his subordinates' advice to forego a frontal assault with the force immediately available to him and sent back to Concord for additional companies before attempting to try a flanking operation to force the provincials to withdraw to the river.

While Smith waited for his reinforcements to march up, Captain Lawrence Parsons was approaching North Bridge with the four companies that had conducted the fruitless search of Barrett's farm. The redcoats had never suspected that the nearby plowed fields were full of weapons and supplies and the frustration of a useless march had yielded, a short time later, to even greater unease when the Regulars heard the sound of gunfire back toward the Concord River.

When Parsons' men arrived at North Bridge the area was nearly deserted, but the bodies of two redcoats were lying on the road near the east end of the bridge and one of the men appeared to have been scalped. The "scalping" had actually occurred well after the confrontation at North Bridge as a teen-aged minuteman hurrying to catch up with his company had been startled when one of the two corpses on the road suddenly sat up and tried to raise himself to his knees. The young colonist reacted to the shock of seeing the "dead" redcoat come to life by smashing his hatchet down on the soldier's skull, producing a grisly wound that looked very much like a scalping. The event was neither premeditated nor authorized but Parsons and his men were convinced that their comrade's death was an act of calculated terror. Their account of the apparent barbarity and cruelty of the provincials would have an enormous impact on the grisly events that would occur on the march back to Boston. Even though the minutemen on the ridge near Concord center had a clear field of fire at Parsons' men when they marched toward the town, the colonials made no attempt to interfere with the redcoats' march, and by 11 A.M. virtually the entire force of Regulars was reunited.

Colonel Francis Smith was a stupid, slow, unimaginative officer, but this otherwise incompetent commander did have enough sense to realize that getting back to Boston would be far more difficult than the outbound march. Smith had already sent a messenger back to Gage requesting substantial rein-forcements, and a more competent leader might have simply deployed his men in good defensive positions around Con-cord and delayed his fallback until the relief force arrived. However, the British colonel apparently continued to under-estimate the fighting capabilities of the colonial militia and he convinced himself that he could march eastward and link up with the reinforcements before the provincials could fully de-ploy against him. Thus just after twelve o'clock on an almost summer-like April afternoon, the British expedition was lined up in Concord center and ordered to march east.

Smith assigned three companies of light infantry to sweep across the high ground north of the Concord-Lexington road with orders to stay ahead of the main column and prevent the colonials from cutting off the route of the march. The remaining 18 companies of grenadiers and light infantry were reorganized for a rapid march through a now openly hostile countryside. The light infantry of the 4th Regiment of Foot had taken such heavy casualties at North Bridge that the survivors were incorporated into other units to provide a little additional firepower for each company. Horse-drawn carts, wagons and carriages were commandeered from the townspeople to serve as ambulances for wounded officers while injured enlisted men would be expected to walk or be left behind to face capture by the colonists. The first mile of the march back toward Boston was relatively uneventful as Smith's flankers were able to discourage the colonials from closing in on the column from the north, while an additional force of light infantry cut across the low, open meadows south of the road to confront any threat from that direction. However, part of the reason for the lack of rebel response in the first stage of the march was that the provincials were actually concentrating further down the road on the other side of the Great Meadows at an ideal ambush site called Merriam's Corner.

Merriam's Corner was a small crossroads settlement dominated by the Merriam farmhouse and its outbuildings which lay astride the intersection of several small country roads, the larger road to Bedford, and the main highway between Concord and Lexington. The multiple country roads had funneled companies from Chelmsford, Reading, Woburn, Billerica, Sudbury and Framingham into a single point of concentration and by one o'clock over 1,100 men were deployed around the buildings and stone walls of the farm. For the first time the provincials could engage the entire British column with the certainty of a numerical advantage, as most of four militia regiments were now in position around the crossroads. The location presented an inviting site for an ambush because the main road narrowed at a bridge over a stream which would force the British flanking companies to come down from the high ground in order to cross Mill Brook, thus sacrificing their ability to discourage rebel flank attacks.

The most advanced position at Merriam's Corner was held by Major John Brooks' battalion of Reading militia. The young doctor-turned-military-officer had deployed his men in a barn and behind a series of stone walls about 100 yards from the bridge. Brooks had planned a surprise attack on the British column, but one or two of his men fired their muskets at extreme range and the redcoats were quickly alerted to a possible ambush. A company of grenadiers was just marching over the bridge when the shots rang out, and the Regulars formed a tight rank and fired a volley which simply sailed over the colonists' heads. The Reading men were ordered to return fire and one British officer and eight enlisted men dropped to the ground dead or wounded. Brooks had no intention of engaging in a stand-up slugging match with bayonet-toting grenadiers and he ordered his men to melt into the woods while the frustrated and decimated redcoats marched over Mill Brook bridge.

The eastern side of the stream was dominated by a series of hilly orchards that were now filled with colonists under the command of Colonel Thomas Nixon, a famous veteran of the French and Indian War. The orchards would have provided an excellent ambush site in high summer, but on this warm April afternoon the trees were still bare and the Regulars could clearly see their antagonists deployed among the trees. Smith ordered several companies of grenadiers to fix bayonets and take the high ground and within minutes the redcoats were bellowing blood-curdling cheers and charging uphill. As the Regulars poured through the largest orchard on Brooks Hill, they were met by a crashing roar of musketry from the Chelmsford militiamen who had been concealed from sight. One provincial sergeant picked off five Regulars by himself and an exasperated Smith was forced to call off the assault and order the men back into line of march with the rebels still firing from the slopes.

Once the British column had emerged from the gauntlet of fire surrounding Merriam's Corner, the Regulars made a rapid advance toward Tanner Brook where the road to Lexington turned sharply to the left. Both sides of the road were dominated by particularly dense woodlands that concealed Major Loammi Baldwin's Woburn battalion on one flank and Major Brooks' highly mobile Reading men on the opposite side. The two battalions held their fire until the light companies of the 4th King's Own and 5th regiments of foot marched into range and then opened a devastating crossfire that decimated the two units within five minutes. British flankers achieved a small measure of revenge when they surprised one rebel firing party from behind and killed or wounded four men. Redcoat losses mounted so fearfully on this stretch of road that it was soon christened "The Bloody Angle" by both sides.

Smith's force was now approaching the boundary between the towns of Lincoln and Lexington and the redcoats were rapidly marching back into the range of Captain Parker's Lexington militiamen. The survivors of Lexington Green took cover along the crest of a rocky hill just over the town line and waited for revenge. As the now sorely pressed Regulars came into sight and drew opposite the hill, Parker gave the order to fire that had eluded him earlier. One of the first Regulars shot was Colonel Smith, who tumbled out of his saddle with a painful thigh wound while several of his staff officers were either more severely wounded or killed in the Lexington men's volley. When he saw his commander go down, Major Pitcairn rode up from the rear of the column and ordered several units of grenadiers to launch a bayonet charge up the slopes of what would later be called Parker's Hill. The redcoats forced the Lexington militiamen to retreat from the crest of the ridge and at least one of the men who was wounded in the morning action, Jedidiah Munroe, was killed in the assault, but the redcoats quickly confronted even heavier rebel fire when they approached an even steeper slope called the Bluff. As the British thrust came to a screeching halt, Pitcairn called up his reserve force of Royal Marines and personally led the sea soldiers in a desperate charge to occupy the provincial defenders while the rest of the now staggering redcoat column pushed through on the road below. Pitcairn was injured when his horse bolted in the confusion and the pressure on the colonial lines rapidly evaporated, leaving the provincials free to concentrate their fire on the Regulars marching along the road.

Participants in the battle on both sides now began to sense that the British march toward Boston was edging closer to a panic-stricken rout than a mere withdrawal as the command structure of the Regulars was rapidly disintegrating. Lt. John Barker admitted that the rebels "were increasing from all parts while ours was reducing from deaths, wounds and fatigue and we were totally surrounded with such incessant fire as it is impossible to conceive, our ammunition was likewise near expended." Ensign de Berniere noted grimly, "when we arrived within a mile of Lexington, our ammunition began to fail and the light companies were so fatigued with flanking that they were scarce able to act, and a great number of wounded, scarce able to get forward, made a great confusion. Colonel Smith had received a wound through his leg, a number of officers were also wounded, so that we began to run rather than retreat in order. We attempted to stop the men and form them two deep, but to no purpose, the confusion increased rather than lessened."

The injuries to Smith and Pitcairn threw the burden of command down to the small group of unwounded junior officers who were now primarily responsible for the survival of the column. In one last desperate gesture, those few remaining captains and lieutenants spread themselves across the road, faced the panic-stricken enlisted men head-on and threatened to shoot or bayonet any man who left the ranks to run. The panic momentarily subsided, but concealed colonials began picking off the few available officers and the cordon across the road began to unravel. After a few minutes' hesitation, the distraught enlisted men began to break ranks in ever increasing numbers and started to run down nearby Fiske Hill into the village of Lexington. A few officers tried one last time to get in front of their men before they all stampeded in panic. De Berniere noted "we presented our bayonets and told the men that if they advanced, they should die. Upon this they began to form under a very heavy fire." An increasing number of redcoats were now either drifting into the surrounding fields or merely sitting by the side of the road, in both cases hoping to surrender to the rebels before they were killed. Even the officers began to admit among themselves that it might be better to surrender than risk annihilation. One officer noted that "had an identifiable American commander been present, we must have laid down our arms or been picked off by the rebels at their pleasure." However, no single provincial officer had yet taken command of the mixed units that now represented dozens of Massachusetts communities and surrender activities focused on one or two redcoats at a time surrendering to one or two militiamen. Just as this stream of capitulations was threatening to turn into a flood, the now panic-stricken Regulars in the lead companies staggered around the final bend in the road to Lexington and were startled to see over a thousand of their comrades drawn up in long crimson lines on the heights east of the village green. The feeling of imminent annihilation almost immediately gave way to relief and even euphoria as the survivors of Concord linked up with their counterparts under the command of Hugh, Earl Percy and his invaluable gunners from the Royal Artillery.

General Hugh Percy (1743-1817)

Hugh Percy was the eldest son of the Duke of Northumberland, one of the five wealthiest men in England. The family's enormous influence secured Percy an ensign's commission at age 16 and a rapid series of promotions that included a lieutenant colonelcy, command of a regiment by age 19, and a post of personal aide-de-camp to King George III by age 21. Percy and the king became close friends, and the young colonel married the daughter of the king's mentor, Lord Bute. By the eve of the American Revolution, Percy held the title of earl, held seats in both the House of Lords and House of Commons and was one of the youngest generals in the British army.

When Earl Percy accepted a posting to America as a brigade commander in 1774, he was affected with severe gout, had terrible eyesight and was debilitated by a number of respiratory ailments. However, when he arrived in Boston he quickly became the focal point of much of Tory society. He rented the house that had formerly been used as the governor's residence, imported several expensive carriages and entertained lavishly at dinners that often included a hundred guests. He was also one of the most popular officers in the British army, as he strenuously opposed flogging his men and believed that a good officer led by example. When his brigade conducted marches and training exercises into the Massachusetts countryside, he insisted on walking with his men and spurned the use of a horse. His generosity toward his enlisted men was legendary in the army. When his unit was posted to America, he personally chartered at his own expense civilian ships to bring all the wives and children of his men to Boston, purchased additional food and supplies for the voyage for his men and their families, and upon arrival in Boston gave every man a gold guinea and a new blanket.

Despite his close relations with the king, Percy strongly supported the rights of the colonists and considered a conflict between the British and Americans to be a disaster to both societies. However, upon arrival in Boston, he became extremely critical of patriot methods of enforcing opposition to British laws, although he maintained a positive view of colonists as a whole. After playing a significant role in the Boston campaign, Percy was promoted to major general and led British columns in the victories at Long Island and Fort Washington. He was then assigned an independent command in Rhode Island where he was criticized by General Howe for his failure to capture Providence. Percy refused to continue to serve under Howe and returned to England in June of 1777, where he was promoted to lieutenant general by the king and succeeded his father as Duke of Northumberland. During the next war with France he was promoted to full general but exercised no further field commands.

CHAPTER IV

The Ring of Fire
The British Retreat from Lexington to Charlestown

The British expedition to Concord had escaped annihilation due to the timely intervention of a relief force that had been set in motion several hours earlier. General Gage had begun planning for the contingency of reinforcing Smith's column even before that colonel had embarked his men on the first stage of their operation. The British general alerted his most senior subordinate, Brigadier Hugh Percy, to have his 1ˢᵗ Brigade ready to march by 4 A.M. on Wednesday morning in case Smith requested support. However, Gage's orders were addressed personally to the brigade's adjutant, Captain Thomas Moncreiffe, who was attending a party when the messenger delivered the dispatch to his quarters. Moncreiffe tumbled into bed several hours later with no idea that he was needed for such an important duty and when a messenger from Colonel Smith arrived at headquarters around dawn, not one reinforcing unit was preparing to march. It took nearly an hour to awaken and deploy 1ˢᵗ Brigade units scattered around Boston, and as the troops were formed up in the street in a shuffling, confused mass of units, another hour was wasted. The already badly delayed mobilization quickly struck another snag when an army officer realized that the anticipated reinforcement of Royal Marines had never arrived. Since the marines were a separate military entity, Gage had sent orders to the Royal Marine battalion commander to prepare his men for a march. But the battalion commander was Major John Pitcairn, who at that moment was somewhere on the road between Lexington and Concord while the orders were sitting unopened in his quarters. Finally, a subordinate officer was located and provided with orders and His Majesty's Marines were hustled out of their barracks to augment a relief column that was now late by an additional 90 minutes. At a few minutes before nine o'clock, almost five hours behind schedule, the 1st Brigade raised its colors, ordered its bandsmen to begin playing, and marched out of Boston toward the Massachusetts countryside.

Hugh, Earl Percy, commanded what was considered the elite brigade in Gage's army; a force that even with the absence of the flank companies, deployed over 1,000 men in three regiments of foot, a Royal Marine battalion, and a Royal Artillery battery. The infantry units included the 4th (King's Own) Regiment, the 23rd (Royal Welsh Fusiliers) Regiment and the 47th Regiment of Foot augmented by a reinforced Marine battalion that was larger than any of the army regiments. Possibly the most important component of this relief column was a pair of Royal Artillery 6-pounder field guns that could provide an edge in firepower that the rebels couldn't easily match in a fluid engagement. In one of Percy's few major mistakes this day, the general rejected the battery commander's request to bring along an additional ammunition wagon which meant that the British guns would be limited to the relatively few cannon balls that could be crammed into the weapons' side boxes. The final element in the relief column was a contingent of Loyalist volunteers who would perform scouting duties and provide vital information about the surrounding countryside while awaiting an opportunity to get revenge on the patriots who had driven many of them from their country houses into the protection of the British guns in Boston.

The men in the relief column probably left Boston in a much more positive frame of mind than their counterparts in the original Concord expedition. First, they were led by a far more popular commander than Colonel Smith; General Percy was one of those rare British officers who detested floggings and actually considered the welfare of his men to be a major concern. Also, these men were not marching through bogs and swamps in the middle of the night and were not under orders to maintain silence. As the men marched along the country roads, the regimental bands played a taunting rendition of "Yankee Doodle" while colonists in the towns of Roxbury, Brookline and Cambridge tightly shuttered their windows. When the column reached Menotomy at shortly past one o'clock, the mood of the men became far more serious. Lt. Edward Gould of the King's Own Regiment had been wounded at Concord and sent back to warn Percy that Smith's column was running into serious trouble and had expended most of its ammunition. The relief commander admitted that the countryside was ideally suited for ambush as "it was covered with stone walls and was beside very hilly, stony country, etc." By the time the reinforcements were half way between Menotomy and Lexington, the Regulars could hear the rising crescendo of a rattle of gunfire and the festive mood of the march evaporated rapidly. When the column reached Munroe's Tavern on the outskirts of the village, Percy ordered his men to halt and deploy along the high ground adjoining the public house. Within minutes a thousand redcoats were formed along a series of hills with the 4th Regiment of Foot concentrated on the north side of the Lexington Road, the 23rd Regiment on the south side and the 47th Regiment and Marines protecting the vital field pieces in the center.

The first visual confirmation that this march was no training exercise occurred when Percy's men caught sight of the disorganized survivors of the Concord expedition trotting along in near panic on the other side of Lexington as clearly visible colonial units harassed their flank and rear. One regiment of provincials was actually in a more organized battle formation than the Regulars and was closing in on Smith's rear when Percy ordered his artillery to open fire. The colonials were startled to see cannon balls dropping in their midst and they ran for cover just long enough to give Smith's men time to stagger into Percy's lines. When the relief force opened its

British columns from Lexington and Concord converge to begin the retreat to Boston, as colonists fire from behind stone walls. (Earle and Doolittle)

ranks to admit their fleeing comrades, Percy noted "they were so much exhausted with fatigue that they were obliged to lie down for rest on the ground, their tongues hanging out of their mouths, like those of dogs after a chase." Smith's men were able to rest inside the protective cordon thrown out by the relief column, but provincial marksmen crept up in small groups to woods and meadows on both sides of the road and used trees and stone fences for cover as they continued to take their toll of Regulars. Percy reacted to the colonial sharpshooting by ordering his gunners to destroy any building that might be used to hide snipers and within moments the town's meetinghouse and several houses were badly damaged by cannon fire. British skirmishers then used this covering fire to duck into a number of houses and barns near the village common and start a series of fires that soon blotted the landscape with smoke.

Percy was reasonably certain that his well-deployed infantry and artillery could keep the rebels at bay in a stationary battle, but this course of action would not get the Regulars back to Boston and he could expect little, if any, additional reinforcement from a Boston garrison that was now almost drained of manpower. The general called his senior officers together in Munroe's Tavern and discussed possible courses of action. The British commander admitted that he was shocked by the size of the colonial force confronting him as "the rebels were in great numbers, the whole country having collected for twenty miles around." The earl remembered sourly that he had ordered spare ammunition wagons left behind to speed up the march, but now his force was deep in hostile country with no reserves of ammunition for either muskets or artillery. Smith's men were almost totally out of cartridges which meant that the 36 rounds per man carried by the relief column would have to be redistributed in such a way that virtually no one would begin the next stage of the march with more than 20 rounds, a supply that could evaporate in one serious firefight. Meanwhile, although his field pieces were still keeping the rebels at bay by peppering the countryside with menacing salvos, the side boxes would soon be empty and the British trump card would then be useless.

Percy did not know it at the time, but Gage had already dispatched two vital ammunition wagons with an escort of one officer and 13 men to provide the retreating column with adequate musket and artillery supplies for the remaining 15 miles of the march. However, as reports of this small convoy reached patriots in Menotomy, the men of the local alarm companies met at Cooper Tavern to plan an operation to prevent the vital ammunition from reaching Percy's column. David Lamson, a grizzled veteran of the French and Indian War, who was described as being either half Indian or half Black, was chosen to command a small force of a dozen overage militiamen in an ambush of the wagon train. Lamson deployed his men behind a banked wall of earth and stone directly opposite the local meetinghouse, and when the wagons reached the building, the gray-haired patriot jumped in front of the lead vehicle and called on the commanding officer to surrender. The British drivers were startled at the audacity of a single old man to order over a dozen of His Majesty's troops to surrender, but when the redcoats refused to capitulate, the well-concealed militiamen poured out a volley of musket fire that dropped the officer, both of the sergeants and half of the enlisted men, while the survivors ran panic-stricken through the woods to the bank of Spy Pond, a half mile south. At this point the totally unnerved redcoats threw their guns into the water and began to walk back toward Boston convinced that hundreds of colonials were closing in on them. When the half dozen survivors came upon an old widow named Mother Batherick, digging up dandelions in a vacant lot, they offered to surrender to her and asked for her protection from the imaginary rebels that they were convinced were deploying to annihilate them. After the old woman gravely conducted her prisoners to the home of a local militia captain, she parted with a warning to the redcoats, "if you live to get back, tell King George that an old woman took six of his grenadiers prisoner." When news of this comic opera surrender reached Britain, opposition newspapers eagerly picked up the theme of the Regulars' timidity and one parliamentary opponent of the North government noted in the House of Commons, "if one Yankee woman can take six grenadiers prisoner, how many soldiers will it take to conquer America?"

While this episode had comic overtones, the actions of a handful of overage colonists ensured that General Percy would be obliged to undertake a return march to Boston with an inadequate supply of ammunition. Percy had already dispatched Lt. Harry Rooke to Gage's headquarters requesting additional troops, but the commanding general refused to strip his already depleted garrison any further; the redcoats deployed around Lexington would have to march back to the sea on their own. The general did agree to ask Admiral Graves to divert two naval vessels up the Charles River to cover the vital bridge at Cambridge, but the remaining British units in Boston would be employed to discourage an uprising among the townspeople that Gage was convinced was about to occur. The 15 miles between Lexington Common and the Charles River were essentially yielded to the ever-growing force of colonial militiamen.

There is no surviving record of Percy's opinion of the military abilities of Colonel Francis Smith, but once the earl took command of the combined columns, he made it clear that he had no intention of continuing the strategy that the colonel had employed from Concord to Lexington. Percy decided to deploy his entire 1,800-man force as a giant mobile British square which would jettison Smith's insistence on an exhaustingly rapid pace and substitute a more deliberate march that would hopefully secure the Regulars' flanks and rear. The relief commander realized that every stone wall and orchard could conceal a rebel firing party, so his first order of business was to keep the colonials pushed back from the road in order to significantly reduce the accuracy of their weapons.

Percy's operational plan was to assign a vanguard force of 50 men to clear the road ahead and shoot any rebels positioned behind the stone fences along the road. The next position in the column would be occupied by the clearly exhausted light infantry and grenadier units who would merely be expected to keep marching and only participate in the battle if any massed rebel force penetrated the redcoat lines. The third segment of the column would be a convoy of carriages, wagons and carts that would carry the wounded men, especially the officers, and would be guarded by six companies of the King's Own and the 47th Regiment of Foot. These vehicles would be followed by the Royal Marines, who would serve as Percy's mobile reserve that could shift back and forth from the north side to the south side of the road in order to solidify whichever flank was more threatened at any particular point along the route. The rear guard would be the Welsh Fusiliers, who would hopefully be able to discourage any attacks from behind by aggressive use of the bayonet, augmented by the artillery pieces if the rebels struck with a massed force.

The most demanding assignments were given to five companies each of the King's Own and 47th regiments who were ordered to protect the flanks by marching overland and striking the rebels from behind whenever possible. These men were told to shoot any adult male they discovered in a house from which rebels were firing and they were encouraged to launch surprise bayonet attacks on any group of provincials who were occupied loading their muskets or were deploying to a new ambush site. This new configuration would maximize Percy's two main advantages of interior lines and more concentrated firepower. The general could shift his reserves from one threatened point to another faster than the provincials could deploy around the outside of the formation and then the Regulars could utilize their well-known ability to fire massed volleys at a rapid pace to decimate any substantial rebel force that made the mistake of bunching up too close to the main column. Percy also raised his men's spirits by promising them that they could enjoy a long respite in the march when they arrived in Cambridge, emphasizing that he did not expect or want the men to exhaust themselves in a rapidly paced march.

Percy's operational plan was a definite improvement on Smith's near disastrous strategy, but the relief force commander still did not fully realize the immense firepower that the provincials were bringing to bear on his vulnerable column. While the earl was finalizing the deployment of his various units, a 38-year-old farmer from Roxbury arrived to take charge of the still fluid colonial forces. Brigadier General William Heath, an overweight, balding country squire was wealthy enough to spend much of his free time discussing military tactics in Henry Knox's Boston bookstore where he browsed through dozens of military treatises and engaged in profitable conversations with British officers who frequented the shop. Now Heath showed up on the Lexington battlefield dressed in a white duster and floppy hat and prepared to engage many of those scarlet-coated acquaintances in a battle that could determine the future direction of the newly initiated war.

Heath was an influential member of the powerful Massachusetts Committee of Safety which had been scheduled to meet that morning in Menotomy, right in the path of the oncoming Regulars. The committee hastily adjourned to Watertown where the members debated the proper colonial response to the now apparent British military initiative. After a two-hour discussion of alternative strategies, Heath and fel-low member Dr. Joseph Warren rode toward Lexington to take command of the provincial units now streaming in from all points of the compass. Heath supervised the re-forming of a regiment that had been broken by the British artillery fire and then led a personal reconnaissance of Percy's position that was conducted so close to enemy lines that a redcoat musket ball tore off part of Warren's wig. After surveying the apparent British order of march, the new American field commander ordered his men to employ a "dispersed though adhering" strategy in which a highly mobile ring of colonial sharpshoot-ers would keep tearing at the flanks and rear of the moving British square while avoiding a massed formation that would allow Percy to fully employ his superior volley fire and artil-lery. The sheer military potential of almost 2,000 British Regu-lars massed in a single formation was an awesome and some-what terrifying sight to Heath and his regimental command-ers, but something over 4,000 colonial militia had arrived in the vicinity of Lexington while messengers informed the gen-eral that additional provincial units were forming along the Charles River to challenge a British retreat into Boston.

Heath soon exhibited many of the most positive charac-teristics of the amateur officers who commanded American forces in a number of Revolutionary War battles. The new field commander calmly yet energetically helped colonels organize their regiments for maximum effect, advised company com-manders on the use of terrain and gave words of praise and encouragement to the rank and file members of the local units. He sent couriers to distant towns to divert their units to block-ing points between Lexington and Boston while deploying his own forces to prepare to strike both British flanks simulta-neously in order to limit Percy's ability to fully utilize his re-serves. While the British companies were formed for the next stage of the march, colonial wagons rolled in from nearby towns loaded with food and ammunition for the thousands of militiamen who were now preparing to challenge Percy's ret-rograde march.

Sometime after 3:30 P.M. the long column of redcoats be-

gan marching eastward on the Boston road and almost immediately the Regulars ran into heavy rebel resistance. Thirty-
five companies of fresh militiamen from Watertown, Medford,
Malden, Dedham, Needham, Lynn, Beverly, Danvers, Roxbury,
Brookline and Menotomy thronged near the roadside and
much of this force now attempted to pierce the British rear.
Eight companies of Welsh Fusiliers withdrew toward the center of the column as each rank fired a concentrated volley and
then leapfrogged over one-another while the Regulars re-
loaded. The successive volleys spewed enormous firepower
at the rebels, but the militiamen quickly learned to duck behind cover at each British order to fire and then pick off the
helpless redcoats as they dropped back to reload. While few
colonials were injured in this exchange, nearly one fourth of
the fusiliers were killed or wounded and Percy rode back just
in time to see his rearguard crumbling rapidly. The British

Engraving from a painting by Alonzo Chappel of the British retreat from
Concord. Terrain, buildings and clothing are very accurate, although the
British and the colonists probably fired at each other from greater dis-
tances.

general pulled the Welsh troops back toward the comparative safety of the wagons and deployed the Royal Marines to check the American thrust. However, aggressive marine bayonet charges usually hit empty air while colonists would suddenly jump up from cover and pick off exposed redcoats. When the count of dead and wounded marines climbed over the 70 mark, Percy was forced to re-deploy the companies guarding the wagons back to the rear. Lt. Frederick McKenzie noted with astonishment the ability of the colonials to mass close enough to inflict heavy losses on the Regulars while dispersing quickly enough to avoid British counter fire. "In our rear, they were most numerous and came on pretty close frequently calling out 'King Hancock Forever.'"

Once Heath confirmed that the attacks on the enemy rear were dissipating Percy's reserves, he started organizing a series of flank attacks designed to begin cutting the British column into ever smaller fragments. Several regiments from Essex and Middlesex started exerting heavy pressure from the north side of the Boston road and gradually pushed Percy's flanking companies back from the adjoining fields and meadows onto the road itself. Provincial regiments were launching sequential attacks as a rotation of companies would open fire and disperse to reload while being replaced by another unit holding loaded muskets and ready to fire. As one British officer exclaimed, "The New England men were much scattered and not about 50 of them could be seen in any one place," yet each relatively small group of rebels seemed to be backed up by a seemingly inexhaustible supply of reinforcements.

The British column was taking heavy casualties but was still reasonably intact when the Regulars emerged from the high ground near Pierce's Hill to the flat countryside that led to the town of Menotomy. This low ground, known locally as the "Foot of the Rocks," contained a more solid concentration of militia units from Roxbury, Dorchester and Brookline, and as Heath noted, "the right flank of the British was exposed to a body of militia . . . until the British had here recourse to their field pieces again; but they were now more familiar than before," and the artillery's ability to terrorize the militiamen was beginning to diminish. The result was a running battle for the next mile and a half until the column reached the Menotomy town center where a whole new pattern of fighting erupted.

Menotomy was a large enough town to contain a relatively densely-populated, central area that now included a number of houses and public buildings occupied by colonial sharpshooters. As the redcoats entered the town, a deadly round of street fighting erupted. Rebel marksmen would pick off Regulars from upper story windows while the British countered by using their field pieces to smash the walls of buildings or sending bayonet-wielding infantrymen charging into the structures to skewer anyone who even appeared to be capable of challenging the column. A dramatic example of this brutal street fighting occurred when 58-year-old Jason Russell escorted his wife and children into a neighboring house and then constructed a breastwork outside of his front door with piles of shingles. At this point a group of provincials came running down the road with a redcoat flanking party behind them and the rebels dashed into Russell's house to make a stand. Russell, who was disabled by a lame foot, was the last to reach his doorway and was wounded by two British bullets as he tried to get behind his improvised breastwork. The Regulars bayoneted the slumping colonial at least a dozen times, smashed through the shingles and started slashing at the fleeing militiamen who had no bayonets of their own. Eight survivors fled into Russell's cellar and shot the first two redcoats who tried to come down after them. However, while these Regulars backed off from a fight to the death with the provincials in the cellar, another part of the redcoat flanking party cornered the rest of the colonials as they fled out the back door of the Russell house and sprinted for cover in his back yard. Almost every militiaman went down with fatal bayonet wounds in a brief, one-sided engagement. Meanwhile, a small force of minutemen from Danvers and Lynn had set up an ambush site in Russell's nearby orchard despite the exhortations from one of their officers that the position was too open to a British flank attack. A few minutes later a redcoat flanking company caught the provincials from the rear and killed almost a dozen men, many of them after they had already surrendered.

The "battle of Menotomy" became the most brutal engagement of the day as house-to-house and room-to-room fighting resulted in Regulars and militiamen clubbing and bayoneting one another, pistols flashing, men swinging tomahawks and hunting knives and dozens of casualties on each side. In one instance a crippled 78-year-old man, Samuel Whitmore, refused to leave his bedroom when warned of the approaching redcoats and armed himself with a musket, two pistols and a cavalry saber. When the British stormed into the room he killed the first man with his musket, shot two more with his pistols and slashed several more with his sword before he was bayoneted 14 times and left for dead in a pool of blood. Neighbors quickly tended to Whitmore's multiple wounds, and he recovered well enough to live to the age of 96. This grisly scene was repeated even more tragically at Cooper's Tavern. In this case no Americans attempted to challenge the British column, but two locals, Jason Winship and Jabez Wyman, insisted on finishing their tankards of ale and owner Benjamin Cooper and his wife Rachel continued to mix batches of flip after the rest of the patrons sought safety from the approaching redcoats. Suddenly a squad of Regulars burst into the tap-room and opened fire. The landlord and his spouse saved themselves by diving into the cellar, but their two customers were shot and then mutilated by the rampaging Regulars. According to Cooper, his patrons were "most barbarously and inhumanely murdered; being stabbed through in many places, their heads mauled, skulls broke and their brains beat out on the floors and walls of the house."

The body count in Menotomy continued to mount as redcoats attempted to burn houses and were overwhelmed by newly-arriving companies of militiamen who were in turn attacked by British flanking parties. At least 25 rebels and 40 Regulars were killed in the town and dozens more were severely wounded by the time the British cleared the community and approached the bridge that linked Menotomy with the north end of Cambridge on the other side of the Menotomy

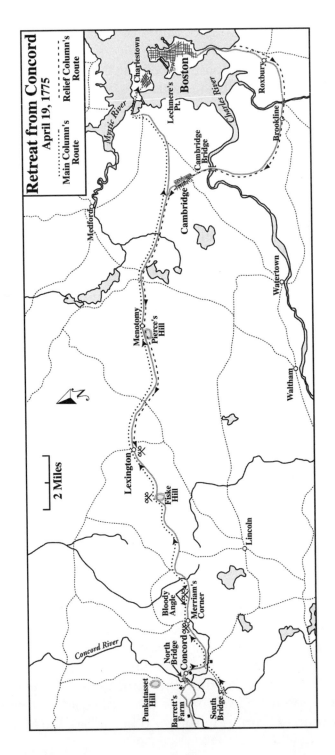

River. As the redcoats crossed the river, a small but resolute band of colonials under Major Isaac Gardner barricaded themselves behind a pile of empty wine casks in the yard of local blacksmith Jacob Watson. Gardner was attempting to delay the British column until other units had time to deploy in Cambridge proper, but a force of redcoat flankers got around the barricade unobserved and another half-dozen patriots were slashed and stabbed to death including their commander, the highest ranking officer killed on either side during the day.

Lord Percy had now forced his way into Cambridge, but his original plan of resting his men before they attempted to reach Boston began to crumble as fresh companies of militiamen harried him on every side. The British commander was also rapidly losing control of his men who were now engaged in an orgy of looting and plundering in each small hamlet they entered. Lt. Barker noted "the plundering was now shameful, many hardly thought of anything else; what was worse, they were now encouraged by some officers." Lt. McKenzie added, "many houses were plundered by the soldiers notwithstanding the efforts of some officers to prevent it. I have no doubt this influenced the rebels, and many of them followed us further than they would otherwise have done." Even one of Gage's staff officers insisted, "I cannot commend the behaviour of our soldiers on their retreat. They began to plunder and paid no obedience to their officers." British soldiers who might have been hanged for stealing a loaf of bread in Boston a week earlier were now carrying even larger loads of clothes, jewelry, tableware and even a church's set of communion silver on their backs and their pace had slowed to a crawl. As word of the looting and senseless murders made its way into the countryside, fresh regiments of provincials began planning a counterattack that would cut off the Regulars from the Charles River and then chew the retreating column into ever smaller pieces until the redcoats had surrendered or were annihilated.

The provincials now had enough units in the field to overwhelm the Regulars but their forces were widely scattered and difficult to contact on short notice. Rebel formations were slashing at the redcoat flanks as Percy's column wheeled toward the Charles River but the Royal Artillery battery was still able to keep the provincials from massing a large enough force to crush the Regulars. By the time the British column had pushed forward to Cambridge's main bridge, the rebels had removed the span's planking and additional regiments were deploying along the access route. General Heath was now convinced that he had a real opportunity to pin the whole redcoat force against the Charles River and perhaps bag the entire column. If the colonials on the scene could surround the redcoats and keep them immobilized, nearly 50 militia regiments could be concentrated for a final assault.

At this point of supreme crisis, Percy made a bold decision that saved the British army from a humiliating disaster in the first battle of the newly initiated war. The general ordered his men to continue to advance toward the skeletal frame of the bridge as if they intended to seize the structure. Dozens of companies of provincials concentrated to deny the bridge to the redcoats. Then, at the last possible moment, Percy ordered an abrupt change of direction for the column and the redcoats sprinted over a narrow road called Kent Lane which the provincials had not bothered to fortify. As the startled rebels attempted to respond to this surprise maneuver, the British general used his interior lines to outmarch his opponents in a dash toward Charlestown and its vital high ground of Bunker Hill and Breed's Hill. The redcoats dashed across Charlestown Neck, the two field pieces fired their last few rounds to hold the colonials at bay, and the Regulars furiously threw up breastworks on Bunker Hill. Pitcairn and his Marines fought a desperate rearguard action on the neck to buy time for the entrenching army units. When the surviving sea soldiers pulled back onto Charlestown Peninsula, newly alerted naval vessels poured covering fire into the rebel pursuers. Percy's bold gamble had turned a possible annihilating defeat into a successful, if costly, retrograde, but by midnight of Wednesday, April 19, the British army was in a virtual state of siege, and the king's authority stretched only a few hundred yards in any direction from Gage's luxurious offices in Province House.

The battles for Lexington and Concord and the subsequent

retreat to Charlestown had cost the British army 73 men killed and 174 wounded which was almost 10 percent of the entire garrison of Boston. The colonial militia had suffered 49 fatalities and 41 injuries, mostly in the opening stage of the battle at Lexington and the closing stage of the battle at Menotomy. During the interval between these two bloody encounters, the provincials had decimated the British column with extremely light losses among their own numbers and on at least one occasion, had almost caused the capitulation of Smith's entire force. While Percy's quick thinking had ultimately saved the redcoat column from annihilation, the British army had suffered a defeat far beyond the loss of almost 300 Regulars in battle. The raiding force had captured or destroyed only a minuscule proportion of available rebel supplies and weapons, thus negating the whole concept of the operation. Beyond this, the British incursion has aroused the entire Massachusetts countryside to resistance and demonstrated to the colonists that Regular troops were not invincible and, in fact, could be decisively defeated under the right circumstances. Captain Parker's insistence that if Britain wanted a war, it should start on Lexington Green had been dramatically proven accurate, and now armed force would determine the dispute between Britain and her American colonies.

General William Heath (1737-1814)

William Heath was one of the few senior American generals during the Boston campaign who had not served in the provincial forces during the French and Indian War. Heath was a wealthy landowner in the Boston suburb of Roxbury at the time of parliamentary passage of the Stamp Act and he responded to the legislation by accepting a commission in an elite Boston artillery company. By the early 1770's, Heath was a noted writer on military issues in Massachusetts newspapers, as he closely observed British Regulars on drills and maneuvers and studied dozens of military textbooks in the evenings. He was particularly interested in adapting military tactics to the peculiarities of the American countryside and he became convinced that provincial troops could defeat British Regulars if they exploited mobility and concealment.

At the time of the outbreak of hostilities, Heath was one of the senior generals in the Massachusetts provincial forces and was recognized throughout the colonies as a leading military scholar. He was given an opportunity to practice his concept of colonial warfare at a series of isolated, semi-independent engagements during the British retreat from Concord to Charlestown, and was subsequently given significant responsibilities under both Artemus Ward and George Washington.

Heath had a mixed record of success after the British evacuation of Boston. He was a division commander during the New York campaign and was instrumental in holding open the American line of retreat in the wake of the British capture of Manhattan. Later in 1776 he refused to accede to General Charles Lee's potentially disastrous order to transfer most of his force defending the Hudson River forts to Lee's personal command in New Jersey. On the other hand, his failure to capture British-held Fort Independence in 1777 was informally criticized by Washington, although Heath was still placed in the high profile role of guarding Burgoyne's surrendered army after Saratoga.

By the time of the Yorktown campaign Heath was one of the most senior major generals in the American army and he utilized that position to begin a successful postwar political career, which included membership in the Massachusetts Convention that ratified the constitution, two terms as state senator and election to the lieutenant governor's chair. His memoirs, published in 1798, emerged as one of the most widely-read personal accounts of the Revolution and when he died in 1814 he was the last surviving major general of the Continental army.

CHAPTER V

The Redcoats under Siege

As night fell on this climactic day in American history, General Percy's troops continued their fortification of Bunker Hill supported by the guns of H.M.S. *Somerset* while colonial officers debated their own options. General Heath briefly considered massing every available provincial regiment and attempting to push the Regulars into the Charles River, but he decided reluctantly that "any further attempt upon the enemy, in that position, would have been futile." The colonial commander fully expected a British counterattack the next morning, quite possibly supported by Gage's entire garrison, so he decided to pull the main body of militia back to the more easily defendable ground around Cambridge, while a small screening force was ordered to deploy along Prospect Hill which dominated access to the Charlestown Peninsula.

Heath need not have worried about a British attack, as Gage and Percy were too stunned by the day's events to consider offensive operations. The elite grenadier and light infantry companies had lost over 25 percent of their men and had not slept for nearly two days, the Royal Marines had spent much of the day launching uphill bayonet attacks that cost almost a fifth of their total strength and the remainder of Percy's units, although more intact than the elite troops, were exhausted by their march and subsequent entrenching activities at Charlestown. The dozens of British wounded were being ferried across the Charles River to Boston in longboats in a time consuming process, while the decimated flank companies waited their turn to be transported across the river for rest and refitting. As the British casualties and flank companies were being evacuated from Charlestown Peninsula, thousands of late arriving colonials who had marched from distant towns began arriving on the scene. When dawn broke on Thursday, April 20, Gage and his senior officers were stunned to discover over 15,000 colonials virtually surrounding the city from Boston Neck to Charlestown Neck. It now became obv`iious to thBritish commanders that while they might have initiated hostilities by the march to Concord, the rebel colonists might be the ones to determine the direction of the next stage of the war. General Percy almost immediately began to warn friends and colleagues in Britain that it would be dangerous to underestimate the American rebels as fighting men. "You may depend upon it, that as the rebels have now had time to prepare, they are determined to go through with it, nor will the insurrection here turn out so despicable as it is perhaps imagined at home. For my part, I never believed, I confess, that they would have attacked the king's troops or have had the perseverance found in them yesterday." General Gage took a more leisurely six days to write a report on the initial battle of the war, but his tone largely supported his subordinate. "The rebels are not the despicable rabble too many have supposed them to be, and find it owing to a military spirit encouraged amongst them for a few years past, joined with an uncommon degree of zeal and enthusiasm." Gage admitted that he was stunned by the difference in military prowess between the colonials he had observed in action in the French and Indian War and the aggressiveness displayed by the Americans in almost annihilating Smith's column. "In all their wars against the French, they never showed so much conduct, attention and perseverance as they do now."

While Gage was composing a leisurely post-mortem of the battle for his superiors in London, the patriot leaders were loading Captain John Derby's fast schooner *Quero* with documents designed to provide Englishmen with the colonial version of events before the royal governor's official dispatches sailed anywhere near the British Isles. On May 27, 1775, two full weeks before the first official dispatches reached London, the colonial view of Lexington and Concord was appearing in sympathetic newspapers in the British capital. The Massachusetts Committee of Safety had engaged in a frenzy of gathering testimony from witnesses to the events including militiamen, civilians and even captured British soldiers and officers. When much of the colonial version of the engagements was supported by an affidavit from a mortally wounded British officer who also praised the humanity of his captors, anti-government feelings reached a crescendo. One supporter of Lord North claimed, "the Bostonians are now the favourites of all the people of good hearts and weak heads in the kingdom. . . their saint-like account of the skirmish at Concord has been read with anxiety and believed." Former royal governor Thomas Hutchinson noted sourly, "the opposition rejoice that the Americans fight after it has generally said they would not, the first accounts were very unfavourable, it not being known that they all came from one side." King George III reacted to the colonial dispatches by emphasizing the probability of enormous exaggeration in the rebels' accounts insisting, "it is not improbable but some detachment sent by General Gage may not have been strong enough to disperse the provincials assembled at Concord, but no great reliance can be given in the manner in which it will undoubtedly be exaggerated by an American newspaper."

When Gage's official reports arrived in the *Sukey* 14 days later, the dispatches presented a very different version of responsibility for the violence on April 19, but provided little solace for the king and his ministers concerning the seriousness of the rebel insurrection. The British commander requested massive reinforcement of his army just to hold the city of Boston and implied that any offensive operations would require the stripping of most garrisons in Britain. The king responded to his general's reports by exclaiming that "the rebellious children will rue the hour that they cast off obedience" and directed Lord North and his ministers to devise a plan to crush the rebellion in one campaign.

The North government initiated an extensive series of policy meetings in which the king's ministers eventually agreed that three broad strategies for conducting an American war were available to them: a significant reinforcement of Gage's army to ensure the military conquest of New England and a crushing of the rebellion at its source; the withdrawal of the army and the imposition of a naval blockade to coerce the provincials into coming to terms with the British government; or the initiation of negotiations with the Continental Congress with the prospect of eliminating most direct taxes in return for voluntary contributions to imperial defense and a maintenance of colonial ties to the empire. However, when the king effectively vetoed the concept of negotiation, the ministry was forced to choose between a primarily military or naval response. By June 15 the ministers had essentially rejected the idea of a naval blockade alone and decided on a number of steps to augment Gage's army for offensive operations.

On the warm summer evening of June 28, 1775, the British cabinet met in a special session to finalize an operational plan to subdue the rebels in Massachusetts. The king's ministers agreed to immediately dispatch four large frigates to Boston to increase the force of Royal Marines in the garrison and to provide additional naval firepower for operations near the city. In addition, a number of military reinforcement plans were authorized. The Royal Highland Regiment (Black Watch) was expanded to 1,000 men and ordered to America; three regiments each from Gibraltar and Minorca would be sent to Gage and replaced by Hanoverian troops in British service; Sir Guy Carleton, royal governor of Canada, was authorized to recruit 2,000 Canadian volunteers and send them to Boston; Indian superintendent Guy Johnson was directed to enlist the aid of the Six Nations of the Iroquois to threaten Massachusetts from the rear; and finally, additional companies of Royal Marines would be raised and sent to Boston.

Gage was notified of the steps being taken to meet his

request for reinforcements and told "from the moment this blow was struck and the town of Boston invested by the rebels, there was no longer any room to doubt the intention of the people of Massachusetts Bay to commit themselves in open rebellion." The British commander was directed "to use every effort, both by land and sea, to subdue the rebellion, should the people persist in the rash measure they have adopted." However, while Gage would receive substantial reinforcements, Lord North and his colleagues now openly questioned whether Gage was the right man to suppress the growing rebellion. The official letter to Gage acknowledging the dispatch of reinforcements also criticized the general's judgment as to whether he had carefully considered the consequences of his expedition to Concord and insisted that the general's report was not sufficiently "full and explicit" to meet the needs of the ministers. Lord Dartmouth sarcastically informed Gage that the imminent arrival of several crack British regiments should not only allow the general to hold Boston, but enable him to begin seizing territory in New York and Rhode Island. The ministers agreed that even if Gage was to be permitted to retain command, the dispatch of generals Howe, Clinton and Burgoyne to America should stiffen the commanding general's resolve and enable one or more of these seemingly more talented and energetic officers to attend to the day-to-day operation of the army.

While the British cabinet authorized a level of reinforcements that would allow Gage to conduct offensive operations, the colonial rebels were working daily to make sure the redcoats remained pinned in Boston. The person most directly responsible for this task was General Artemus Ward, the new commanding general of the Massachusetts provincial army. Ward had been appointed to the position in November of 1774 when Jedidiah Preble had rejected the post due to age and ill health. On the morning of April 19, Ward had been suffering from a recurring case of bladder stones when a messenger galloped into Shrewsbury with the news of the British expedition against Concord. The decidedly middle-aged general, still shaking with excruciating pain, mounted a horse and raced for Cambridge to direct the deployment of provincial units while William Heath assumed responsibility for field operations. After the British retreat into Charlestown, Ward established headquarters in the Jonathan Hastings house which was also the office of the Committee of Safety. The general quickly developed an effective working relationship with his fellow Committee of Safety members as they attempted to confront two daunting challenges in the aftermath of Lexington and Concord.

The first problem was the need to prepare a still largely decentralized army to repulse a possible British offensive that could be inaugurated at almost any time. While Gage was initially satisfied to merely defend Boston, the provincials were convinced that the British were actively preparing a major offensive somewhere along the vast expanse of fortifications ringing the city. Ward countered this threat by dividing his army into three relatively autonomous wings that could mobilize quickly to challenge a redcoat sortie in their sector. The American general believed the most likely British attack would come from Boston Neck toward the provincial lines in Roxbury. Defense of this right wing of the Yankee line was entrusted to the colony's most popular and experienced militia commander, Brigadier General John Thomas. Thomas was an energetic, talented leader who quickly constructed a formidable system of fortifications anchored by the Charles River. William Heath assumed initial responsibility for the right wing of the colonial line which included fortifications running from Prospect Hill across the Mystic River to Chelsea. However, when members of the Committee of Safety became convinced that Gage intended to launch an offensive across Boston Neck against the colonial lines in Roxbury, Heath was ordered to take four regiments and augment Thomas' wing of the army. Meanwhile, Ward retained direct command of the center of the provincial army. By late April the Shrewsbury native was responsible for an enormous 12-mile arc of fortifications that stretched from Roxbury to Chelsea.

Ward's second significant challenge was the unenviable task of feeding and supplying a makeshift army that had no commissary, no quartermasters and not even an accurate count of its strength. Individuals and even entire companies wandered in and out of camp every day, rendering the estimate of 15,000 provincial troops more like 10,000-12,000 available at any given moment of crisis. Ward arranged for every nearby town to supply food to the army on a regular basis while a number of units received provisions from their own communities. However, few reserve supplies were stockpiled and no one had any idea how long the siege would last. What might seem like an exciting adventure to a provincial farmer manning the lines for the first week or two of the siege often became an unacceptable burden when that farmer realized that his wife and children could not operate the farm for long in his absence. Thus it was imperative that some tangible progress should be made that might convince the colonial militiamen that they were not committed to an interminable stalemate. Luckily for Ward and his officers a combination of British carelessness and Yankee energy produced the first glimmer of hope that Boston would not remain in redcoat hands indefinitely.

The day after the British retreat from Concord, General Gage and Admiral Graves held an emotional meeting to consider their response to the new rebel threat. Graves was a corrupt, incompetent naval commander, but he did possess substantial insight into the strategic dilemma facing His Majesty's forces in Boston. The admiral urged his military counterpart to burn Charlestown and Roxbury to the ground and fortify the two principal heights that overlooked Boston, Bunker Hill near Charlestown Neck and Nook's Hill in Dorchester near Boston Neck. While Nook's Hill was currently unoccupied, Bunker Hill was held by elements of the 2nd and 3rd Brigades who were just now in the process of extending the fortifications thrown up by Percy's men the night before. Gage disagreed with Graves on almost every point. The royal governor was convinced that the patriots had cleverly plotted to leave thousands of rebel sympathizers behind in Boston with orders to strike the Regulars from behind while the provincial militia launched a frontal assault. Thus a wide dispersal

British sketch of Boston as seen from Breed's Hill. Clearly visible at right is Copp's Hill, where Clinton and Burgoyne watched the early stages of the battle of Bunker Hill.

of his fewer than 3,000 available unwounded soldiers could leave the Regulars wide open to annihilation. Instead of following the admiral's advice, he ordered Boston Neck closed and an artillery battery deployed to protect the city against an attack from Roxbury; he asked Graves to place several warships near the neck to supplement his own cannons; and 6-pounder naval guns were fitted to flatboats to serve as floating batteries on the Charles River adjacent to Boston Common where the water was too shallow for conventional ships.

The reinforcement of the defenses opposite the rebels in Roxbury was primarily accomplished through a corresponding and highly controversial decrease in the British deployment around Charlestown Peninsula. In one of his most significant blunders of the campaign, not only did Gage fail to fortify Dorchester Heights, a lapse that would come back to haunt the British army the next March, but also the growing number of men and fortifications on Bunker Hill was totally reversed when the commanding general ordered the whole force of Regulars on Charlestown Peninsula evacuated to defend Boston proper. These units were redeployed along with a battery of heavy 28-pounder naval guns on the summit of Copp's Hill while other units were dispatched to shore up British positions on Fort Hill and to augment Major Pitcairn's Royal Marine garrison on Boston Common. Finally, a newly raised regiment of Loyalist volunteers under Colonel Timothy Ruggles was deployed in strategic areas around the city to provide early warning of the expected rebel uprising among the citizenry of Boston. By early May Gage felt reasonably confident that he could successfully counter the two most likely colonial threats: an uprising within the city or a frontal assault from Roxbury toward Boston Neck. But the Massachusetts rebels and their growing array of New England allies had no intention of accommodating the British general on either scenario.

One of the most significant developments in the Boston campaign between the engagement at Concord in April and the battle of Bunker Hill in June was the expansion of the rebel army from an almost exclusively Massachusetts body to a regional force including all four of the New England provinces.

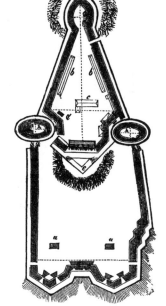

Plan of the British redoubt on Bunker Hill built after the retreat from Lexington and Concord. A substantial structure, it had a magazine, barracks, and a guard house, and could accommodate six cannon.

The genesis of this expanded organization, popularly called the Grand American Army, began to crystallize within hours of the confrontation on Lexington Common. The first tangible support for the patriot cause from outside Massachusetts occured when a courier galloped into Pomfret, Connecticut with news of the fighting at Lexington and Concord. General Israel Putnam was plowing one of his fields when the messenger rode into town. Within minutes the veteran of the French and Indian War summoned his son from an adjoining field to take over his plow, ran nearly a mile to his barn, saddled his best horse, and rode almost continuously until he reached Cambridge, 100 miles away. The Connecticut officer arrived in time to attend Artemus Ward's first council of war and in honor of his immediate offer of assistance, the password along the American lines that night was "Putnam." The almost legendary Connecticut warrior remained in camp long enough to provide his expertise on the deployment of the Massachusetts regiments, and then answered an urgent message from his own legislature to return to Hartford to supervise the mobilization of the Connecticut militia regiments. Putnam then returned to Cambridge to accept Ward's commission as second in command of rebel forces and assumed field command of the central sector of the colonial lines from the Charles River to Lechmere Point directly across from Boston Common.

Putnam's reaction to the news of Lexington and Concord was duplicated by another legendary French and Indian War veteran in New Hampshire. Colonel John Stark was working in his sawmill in Derryfield when a messenger brought news of the events in Massachusetts. Ten minutes later the veteran of the legendary Rogers' Rangers was on his way toward the seacoast while stopping just long enough to direct his subordinates to mobilize his New Hampshire regiment and follow him as soon as possible. Ward promptly gave the newly arrived colonel command of the left wing of the army, which entailed defense of the area from Charlestown Neck to Chelsea and included a number of islands that would soon be contested by both armies.

When news of the fighting in Massachusetts reached the Rhode Island assembly meeting in Providence, that colony's provincial government appointed a committee to arrange for the defense of New England in cooperation with the other provinces. True to Rhode Island's reputation for encouraging religious diversity, command of the colony's three active militia regiments had been parceled out to an Episcopalian and two rival denominations of Congregationalists, but no one could decide which denomination should have the honor of brigade commander. The chief beneficiary of this impasse was Nathanael Greene, a wealthy Quaker anchor maker who had spurned his sect's pacifism by joining an elite militia company and conducting frequent trips to Boston to visit Henry Knox's popular bookstore.

Greene had enlisted as a private in the Kentish Guards but his popularity, and prospects, soared when he returned from a foray into Boston with a cache of badly needed muskets accompanied by a British deserter who the Quaker merchant hired to become the company's drill master. The anchor maker's military activities promptly got him expelled from his Quaker meeting, but also gained the attention of the provincial assembly who now believed they had discovered their compromise candidate for brigade commander. Thus Nathanael Greene accomplished a spectacular promotion from private to general in one leap and the new brigadier quickly utilized his ample funds to turn the Rhode Islanders into the best-equipped, best-uniformed, best-armed unit in the New England army. The brigade's camp on Jamaica Plain became a model for the rest of the army as it featured orderly rows of crisp white tents, straight company streets, and well-armed sentries marching at their posts in a very military manner. When the newly appointed commander of the Continental army arrived a few weeks later, the commander of the Rhode Island brigade would receive special attention in the search for talented senior officers.

Once the Massachusetts provincial army had evolved into a more broad-based New England army, the problems of supply and command became more complicated. Each colony ultimately developed its own supply organization that furnished its units with food, ammunition and other equipment, although few companies had specific uniforms. Artemus Ward was officially the commander of only the Massachusetts regiments but eventually New Hampshire placed its army under his command while Connecticut and Rhode Island allowed their senior officers to copy Ward's orders and send them on to their own troops. While this somewhat loose confederation of the regiments of four colonies continued to present some of the disadvantages of divided command, the alliance also gave a clear message to Gage and the British government that they faced more than an isolated single rebel province and that there remained the distinct possibility that in the not too distant future the armies of four colonies would swell to include regiments from all 13 mainland, English-speaking colonies.

By the middle of May the Grand American Army had stabilized at about 15,000 men which included 11,500 Massachusetts troops, 2,300 men from Connecticut, 1,200 men from New Hampshire and 1,000 Rhode Islanders. The senior officers from each colony began to agree that the men were becoming increasingly bored with the existing stalemate and morale would be improved by a series of offensive maneuvers. The first of these actions occurred on May 13 when General Putnam, accompanied by a squad of fifers and drummers, led a column of 2,200 men from Cambridge, crossed Charlestown Neck and marched through the deserted streets of the abandoned Charlestown to Breed's Hill. From this position the column then marched down to the ferry landing, massed along the shore and began a sarcastic round of cheers for the British sailors watching from nearby warships. After brandishing their muskets and launching into an orgy of yelling and cheering, the large force formed back into ranks and marched back to Cambridge in full view of the startled British garrison. A British officer noted sourly "this afternoon between two and three thousand of the rebels came from Cambridge, marched over the neck at Charlestown and up the heights above the town where they kept parading a long time, then marched into the town and after giving a war whoop opposite the *Somerset* returned as they came."

While this Yankee "offensive" was a bloodless demonstration, four days later the sparring turned far more serious. On May 17 a British barge closed in on the American position at Wheeler's Point and a party of Yankee sharpshooters promptly opened fire, killing two sailors. Ward was certain that the skirmish would provoke major retaliation and 400 men were ordered to set up an ambush at Lechmere Point in case the redcoats attempted to ferry an attack force across the Charles River. At this point Gage was more interested in obtaining additional food supplies than making a mere show of force, and the next probe was not directed at American fortifications but rather at a huge supply of hay stored on Grape Island, seven miles southeast of the city. On Sunday morning, May 21, two British sloops and an armed schooner disembarked a large party of Regulars who were under orders to commandeer as much hay as possible and then burn the rest. While the redcoats were loading the bales on their ships, militiamen in nearby Weymouth discovered the presence of the British and sent a request to General Thomas for help. Three companies of reinforcements were rushed to the village but by the time sufficient boats had been found to ferry the provincials to the island, the Regulars had sailed off with a large supply of hay and an appetite for further raiding expeditions.

Ward and his allied commanders now assumed that the raid on Grape Island was the first in a series of British foraging expeditions and colonial units were soon being assigned to make their own pre-emptive raids on peripheral supply depots to prevent vital food or equipment from falling into enemy hands. On Saturday, May 27, a detachment of 40 New Hampshire troops under John Stark waded over from Chelsea to Noddles Island and Hog Island with orders to drive the livestock from both places back to the mainland before British raiding parties could pounce again. By 11 A.M. one detachment of colonials was rounding up cows, sheep and horses on Hog Island while a second unit was setting fire to two Loyalist-owned houses on Noddles Island and killing the Tories' live-stock. Lookouts posted in one of the British naval vessels quickly spotted the operation, and within 30 minutes a de-tachment of Royal Marines came wading ashore on Noddles Island to drive off the rebels. The 40 Marines were supported by an armed schooner and an armed sloop and the combined firepower of the ships' guns and Marine muskets forced the smaller colonial detachment to sprint into the safety of a ditch and hug the ground for cover. However, when the redcoats formed a skirmish line and advanced across the island, the New Hampshire troops suddenly popped up from cover and poured a volley into the Regulars that killed or wounded al-most a quarter of the force.

Stark, who was in personal command of the Noddles Is-land detachment, used the temporary confusion of the British marines to order his men back to Hog Island to link up with the remainder of the raiding party. The tide was now coming in, and the men were forced to navigate through water up to their chins while the reformed marines opened fire. As bullets kicked up bursts of spray all around them, the detachment waded onto Hog Island while Stark sent one of his men to General Ward for reinforcements. Meanwhile the British brought up additional naval vessels and used their ample supply of guns to keep Stark and his men pinned down throughout the rest of the afternoon. Just before sunset, the British suffered a potentially severe loss when the armed schooner *Diana*, attempting to maneuver closer to the Hog Is-land shoreline, ran aground in shallow water about 60 yards off the beach.

At this point in time Israel Putnam arrived from Cam-bridge with 300 Connecticut troops, accompanied by Dr. Jo-seph Warren who wanted a first-hand view of the growing confrontation. The energetic Putnam led his men across the water from Chelsea to Hog Island, noted the presence of the *Diana*, and promptly waded out to the schooner and shouted for the captain to surrender his vessel. Putnam's demand was rebuffed by two cannon balls that whizzed over his head; but in turn the British captain assumed that the Yankees would soon attempt to board his ship and he gave orders to burn the vessel and evacuate the crew. The captain set fire to the ship and left with his men, not waiting to see whether the flames really succeeded in destroying the vessel. The next morning Putnam made another reconnaissance and was startled to see the schooner substantially intact. A platoon under Captain Isaac Baldwin was dispatched to salvage all usable equipment which included 16 valuable cannon and a number of undamaged sails. Admiral Graves was infuriated at the idea of abandoning a still usable vessel to the rebels and a short time later a reinforced naval squadron and a large force of marines returned to attack the colonials on Hog Island while an attempt was made to turn the schooner back to Boston. Two American field pieces deployed on the shoreline at Chelsea scored enough hits to disable another British ship, which largely neutralized the Royal Navy's success in towing the *Diana* to safety. By the time the British forces withdrew to Boston the "Battle of Noddles Island," as the engagement was labeled, had cost the redcoats almost 50 casualties and two badly damaged ships compared to a trifling colonial list of four men wounded. Both Stark and Putnam were now identified as energetic, heroic leaders and the Connecticut militia commander was promoted to major general for his role in the engagement.

The action around Hog Island had added four 4-pounder cannon and 12 lighter naval swivel guns to the colonists' array of artillery pieces, but even this fairly substantial addition left the rebels desperately short of the heavy guns that were vital in any sort of 18th-century siege. The provincials had been able to establish a ring of fortifications around Boston but none of the American generals was confident that Gage could be kept at bay if he used his vastly superior field artillery and naval guns to attempt to blast his way out of the colonial lines. Artemus Ward and his colleagues from the other provinces were soon spending much of their time attempting to formulate a plan to equalize the disparity between British and Yankee artillery strength. A potential solution to the problem began to emerge from the advice of a little known Connecticut militia captain who developed a plan to secure a huge cache of British artillery for the rebels. Captain Benedict Arnold was a former pharmacist who commanded an elite company of Connecticut troops called the Governor's Foot Guards. Arnold had established himself in relative luxury in the commandeered home of a Cambridge Tory but the mercurial officer was quickly bored by the routines of a siege and was determined to find more exciting duties. Eventually, he met with Joseph Warren and the Committee of Safety and proposed a daring plan for a rebel assault on Fort Ticonderoga, the British bastion in northern New York. If the committee would give him a commission in the Massachusetts provincial army and a regiment of men to lead, he would capture the stronghold and add a large array of guns to the colonial inventory. On May 3, 1775, the committee promoted Arnold to colonel and authorized him to go to western Massachusetts to recruit 400 men for the enterprise. However, by the time the apothecary reached Stockbridge, he began receiving reports that a rival expedition was already headed to Ticonderoga for the same purpose. The new colonel ordered his staff officers to remain behind to recruit the regiment while Arnold himself proceeded alone to intercept a New Hampshire officer named Ethan Allen.

Ethan Allen was probably one of the few men in the colonies who could match Benedict Arnold's unique combination of energy, self-importance, feelings of persecution and short temper. Allen had grown up in the tough frontier area called the New Hampshire Grants and combined an academic career preparing for admission to Yale with regular brawls in local taverns. Allen had become leader of a local gang called the "Green Mountain Boys," a group of hell-raisers who were engaged in an undeclared war with the New York authorities over title to the no-man's land between the two provinces. The outbreak of hostilities between Britain and the colonists provided even more opportunities for action and reward, and by the time Arnold arrived in Burlington, Allen had 250 men ready to march on Ticonderoga. The leader of the Green Mountain Boys refused to accept Arnold's authority over him but was willing to allow a sharing of command between the two men. When the assault force reached the Lake George shoreline

*Fort Ticonderoga at the time of the
Revolution. The main entrance is (a).*

opposite Ticonderoga, the two colonels discovered that boats were available to carry only 83 men, which seemed far too small a unit to capture one of the most important strongholds in the British Empire.

If the American force was small, the number of redcoat defenders was positively tiny: a scratch force of only 40 men, most of them either retired on half-pay or physically unfit for active field service. The American colonels were positive that this key post was far more extensively defended than it actually was, and Allen felt obliged to encourage his men with a dramatic address. "This is a desperate attempt which none but the bravest now dare undertake. I do not urge it on any contrary to his will. I now propose to advance before you in person to conduct you to the gate." However, the British post was hardly on a wartime footing as the main gate was wide open and guarded by only one dozing sentry who ran back into the fort as soon as he spotted the Yankee attackers.

The colonials burst into the fort and deployed along the parade ground while Arnold and Allen charged up the stairs to capture Ticonderoga's commander. The senior officer, Captain William Delaplace and his adjutant, Lt. Jocelyn Feltham tried to bolt the door of the headquarters office while Allen screamed "come out of there you damned old rat" as he

George III in the robes of the Order of the Garter. By contrast, his day-to-day dress was as plain as that of the American merchants who were his opponents.

pounded on the office door. When Feltham responded by asking under what authority these men were invading the king's property, the huge rebel colonel bellowed "in the name of the Great Jehovah and the Continental Congress." Delaplace promptly handed his sword over to the two provincial leaders while a brief firefight on the parade ground below ended with one slight casualty on each side. The capture of 40 marginal redcoats would hardly turn the course of the erupting war, but the huge stone citadel also yielded 120 iron cannon, two brass cannon, 50 swivel guns, two 10-inch mortars, 30 gun carriages, 10 tons of musket balls and 10 cases of powder, the largest single stockpile of artillery in North America. If the rebels could ever manage to transfer any significant number of these guns to the lines around Boston, the British position might well become untenable. Before any serious consideration could be given to transporting this new prize, however, the colonial army at Cambridge would face a British counterattack of almost legendary proportions.

Boston on the Eve of War

The city of Boston in 1775 was the third largest community in the American colonies, with a population of 16,000 compared to New York's 25,000 and Philadelphia's 30,000. Boston's population had passed the 15,000 mark during the 1730's and then predominantly stagnated while the two rival cities were growing rapidly. At the time of Lexington and Concord, Boston was a pear-shaped peninsula containing only 800 acres of primarily hilly land that was surrounded by water. The only connection to the mainland was a narrow marsh called Boston Neck which flooded during heavy rainstorms and was swept by spray even in fair weather. The town was dominated by a number of hills including Copp's Hill, Fort Hill, Cotton Hill and Beacon Hill, and was reputed to have the narrowest, most winding streets of any community in America. Most private dwellings were made of wood, which made the city extremely vulnerable to British threats to burn the town to the ground if the patriots made a serious attempt to capture it.

The most militarily significant feature of 18th-century Boston was its massive series of wharves along the southern side of the town which extended as far out as a half mile into the water and provided docking and repair facilities for dozens of ships at a time. The city was the largest ship-building center in the British empire, and possibly the world, as one-third of all British ships were constructed in the community. The strategic importance of the city was reflected in the firepower of Admiral Graves' American squadron, which carried a total of over 350 guns and over 2,000 seamen. This impressive naval force, combined with General Gage's land based forces and a large contingent of Royal Marines, meant that by the spring of 1775 there were actually more British military personnel stationed in Boston than adult male civilians living in the city.

Impact of the Siege of Boston on Civilians

The siege of Boston was relatively unusual in the sense that most of the civilians in the town were in sympathy with the besieging army, not the defenders. While most of the patriot leaders had left town before the Concord raid, most ordinary citizens remained behind in their homes and shops. Soon after the colonial troops surrounded the city, General Gage, who was obsessed with the possibility of a civilian uprising, began encouraging residents to leave town. Gage negotiated an informal agreement with the Massachusetts Committee of Safety under which anyone could leave Boston with all the possessions they could carry providing that the evacuees turned in any weapons and agreed to refrain from joining the colonial army. In turn, all Loyalist sympathizers could cross Boston Neck with no interference from patriot forces.

A steady stream of civilians crossed Boston Neck into Roxbury after leaving 1,800 muskets, 600 pistols and 1,000 bayonets with British sentries. However, after April 30, leaving the city became progressively more difficult. Boston's Tory leaders were convinced that once most of the patriot sympathizers had evacuated the city, rebel forces would feel free to either bombard the town or attempt to burn the place through incendiary teams. Gage was convinced to gradually tighten evacuation conditions. First, most property had to be left behind, then at least one member of a family had to remain behind and finally, only people who were very poor or were infected with smallpox were allowed to leave. Thus something like 7,000 civilians were ultimately trapped in the city, becoming virtual hostages to the British army.

The interaction of over 10,000 redcoats and 7,000 mostly hostile civilians in a largely besieged city began to create increasing tensions and small-scale violence. In response Gage, and his successor, William Howe, imposed a martial law system that maintained a tenuous peace. While ample supplies of rum were available during the siege, and produced volatile conditions for conflict, most encounters were limited to the trading of insults and to minor vandalism on the part of British troops. Enlisted men who entered occupied private homes without permission were usually brutally flogged or executed. At one point Howe authorized the provost marshal

to go on his rounds attended by an executioner with orders to hang on the spot the first man he discovered stealing combustible materials from a private dwelling.

The besieged population included a sizeable minority of Loyalists who gradually developed a growing number of militia units. Former Massachusetts militia colonel Timothy Ruggles organized a number of loyal companies including the Loyal American Associators, the Loyal Irish Volunteers and the Royal Fencible Americans. These units provided internal security in the town and drilled regularly to meet an all-out rebel assault. The Tories also mingled socially with the British officer corps that sponsored a wide variety of dances and plays that had heretofore been banned in Boston. One of the most heavily publicized productions was called "The Blockade of Boston." It satirized Washington and his soldiers and featured widely distributed handbills which invited the American commander to the premiere and requested him to bring his own noose for his execution. Washington responded to this "invitation" by planning a large scale raid on the British defenses on Bunker Hill just as the curtain was going up on the performance. The result was an engagement that bordered on comedy as British officers still dressed as women rushed to beat off the attack still wearing their petticoats and lipstick.

King George III's "Declaration of War"

Since the American colonies were legally part of the British Empire, a formal declaration of war was not necessary in order to initiate military operations. However, at the opening of a new session of parliament on October 26, 1775, King George issued a Proclamation of Rebellion which, in effect, placed the colonies outside the protection of the British government. The Proclamation declared that "a rebellious war" was being carried out by insurgent colonists for the purpose of separating the American provinces from the rest of the empire. The king insisted that the spirit of the British nation was too high and its resources too numerous to give up such valuable possessions, which had been "planted with great industry, nursed with great tenderness and protected with much expense, blood and treasure." The monarch declared that it was a matter of both wisdom and clemency to put a speedy end to the disorders in America by the most decisive exertions possible. Thus the king called on parliament to enlarge the size of the army and navy, begin negotiations with European governments to hire their troops for use in the colonies, and "set in motion all possible actions that would end the unnatural rebellion."

The king's October speech in essence eliminated any possibility of producing a compromise settlement between parliament and congress before the arrival of the huge British expeditionary force under the command of Admiral Richard Howe. The Proclamation effectively rejected the Continental Congress' "Olive Branch Petition" adopted on July 8, 1775, which requested the king to appoint a peace commission to "restore harmony between Britain and her colonies." The Proclamation of Rebellion ensured that no matter which side emerged victorious at the end of the Boston campaign, a much larger and deadlier round of fighting would emerge in New York sometime in the summer of 1776.

CHAPTER VI

Prelude to Bunker Hill

While rebels and redcoats jockeyed for position in the lines between Boston and the mainland, H.M.S. *Cerebus* was sailing toward Massachusetts with tangible evidence of the British government's determination to crush colonial rebellion. The vessel was carrying a trio of British generals who had been dispatched by Lord North to assist General Gage and coordinate the arrival of the stream of reinforcements that would be making its way across the Atlantic Ocean. Generals William Howe, Henry Clinton and John Burgoyne represented what was considered to be the most talented group of senior officers that Whitehall could assign to the American crisis in that tumultuous spring of 1775. Yet, each man harbored significant reservations about the wisdom of using military power to force the colonists to accept ministerial authority over their internal affairs.

There is little doubt that General Gage would have vastly preferred an additional three infantry regiments instead of a trio of subordinate officers who were actually serving as thinly disguised spies for the prime minister, but the royal governor warmly welcomed his fellow generals and discussed the most effective use of the promised reinforcements. A convoy of troop transports brought a welcome augmentation to the Boston garrison, as three regiments of foot, a regiment of light dragoons, a battalion of Royal Marines, and several batteries of Royal Artillery were landed in the city. The fresh troops were accompanied by four additional British warships to provide expanded naval support. By early June the British garrison had expanded to just under 7,000 men, approximately double the number of redcoats available to Gage at the time of the expedition to Concord. Equally important, more colonial militiamen were currently going home than arriving, so that the 16,000 men facing Gage a few days after the retreat from Lexington had shrunk to about 11,000 in the first week of June. Therefore, the nearly 5 to 1 manpower superiority the rebels enjoyed in the aftermath of the first battle of the war was now closer to a 3 to 2 advantage, a thin margin for a force of amateurs confronting a professional army.

Thomas Gage was an innately cautious commander, but he began to come around to the aggressive attitudes shared by his newly-arrived subordinates. They emphasized the need to push the rebels back into the Massachusetts countryside while making a thrust toward the provincials' almost irreplaceable cache of supplies at Cambridge. The royal governor's councils of war with Howe, Clinton and Burgoyne produced an audacious plan designed to trap the rebels in a huge pincers that would roll up their lines from two directions and send the survivors scurrying into the countryside to be dealt with at the king's pleasure. The emotional discussions in the conference room at Province House produced a plan in which a British detachment would move out against Dorchester Neck, throw up two redoubts on Dorchester Heights and then attack the rebel post at Roxbury. Once Boston was safe from attack in that direction, Howe would lead a large assault force across the Charles River to Charlestown and either attack the American center in Cambridge or outflank their position and cut off their line of retreat toward the west. Even if the coordinated assaults did not bag the entire provincial army, the rebels would lose their supplies, their ammunition and their already meager artillery park, and be rendered incapable of offensive action until Gage received additional reinforcements to actively pursue them. The operation was set to begin on the morning of June 18 with Howe leading the Charlestown assault, Clinton directing the follow up attack on Cambridge and Burgoyne responsible for operations around Boston Neck. With any luck, by nightfall of the 18th, the initiative in the colonial insurrection would have passed to the king's forces and Lord North's plan for substituting colonial "contributions" to the imperial budget in place of direct taxation could be introduced to a chastened and attentive American populace.

The plan that emerged from the British councils of war was a good one, but it was based on the assumption of an element of surprise and passivity of colonial response that simply was not about to happen. The British generals finalized their operational plans on June 12, and by the next morning reports of an imminent redcoat offensive began filtering into colonial headquarters in Cambridge. Artemus Ward and the senior members of the Committee of Safety took the warnings of patriot sympathizers quite seriously and the Provincial Congress meeting five miles away in Watertown was advised to take precautions in case of a full-fledged offensive by the enemy Regulars. Ward's first concern was the diminished size of the colonial army holding the long crescent of entrenchments along the mainland. The original reorganization plan for the provincial forces had envisioned enlisting 20 regiments of 590 men each to serve until the end of the year. The projected goal of 13,600 Massachusetts recruits had not come close to being met and the Bay colony could field only 7,500 men by mid-June, only slightly more than the British garrison in Boston. Ward had also assumed that the other New England colonies and the provinces further to the south would contribute 25 to 30 regiments by the end of summer, but so far, the "continental" component of the "Grand American Army" was limited to two regiments each from New Hampshire, Rhode Island and Connecticut, which added only 3,500 men to the colonial field army.

The British army that the rebels would be facing in the near future could now deploy 13 regiments of foot, 1 regiment of light dragoons, and 2 heavily overstrength battalions of Royal Marines that could each field the equivalent of two infantry regiments. This Regular force was supplemented by the equivalent of a regiment of Loyalist volunteers which included a number of senior officers from the old Massachusetts militia organization. Thus a British offensive campaign could deploy the equivalent of 19 regiments against a rebel force of 26 regiments, a situation that provided little margin for error for the colonials. This margin was made even thinner by the disparity in artillery between the opposing armies. By the middle of June only 24 pieces of field artillery were available to the provincials while the combined firepower available to the Royal Navy and Royal Artillery amounted to just over 240 guns, a staggering 10-to-1 advantage. Therefore, unless the colonials could seriously disrupt Gage's operational plan, it was reasonable to assume that a spirited and properly implemented British offensive had the manpower and firepower to have an excellent chance of achieving its objectives.

Artemus Ward, much like Thomas Gage, was a cautious, conservative commander who harbored a basic instinct to simply maintain his current deployment of forces until the expected British offensive produced a clear-cut pattern of intentions. However, Ward was answerable to a Provincial Congress that contained a number of influential members who had no intention of allowing the redcoats to smash into the colonial positions with little initial hindrance. The Congress directed that "as it appears of importance to the safety of this colony that the hill called Bunker's Hill in Charlestown be securely kept and defended, therefore, resolved unanimously that it be recommended to the Council of War that the aforementioned Bunker's Hill be maintained by sufficient force being posted there." Ward might still have an opportunity to fight the Regulars in a battle around Cambridge, but only after the first set-piece battle of the war was contested on ground that the commanding general most emphatically wanted no part of defending.

General Ward obeyed the Provincial Congress' directive to fortify Bunker Hill, but he assigned a relatively small force to accomplish the task. While several Connecticut and New

Hampshire regiments were already deployed near Charlestown Peninsula in a wide arc between Inman's Farm and Charlestown Neck, most of these units would be held in their current positions while three Massachusetts regiments were ordered from the main camp in Cambridge to fortify the high ground about Charlestown. These regiments, under the overall command of Colonel William Prescott and led by Prescott, Colonel Ebenezer Bridge, and Colonel James Fry, would be augmented by a 200-man detachment of Connecticut troops under Captain Thomas Knowlton and a 4-gun artillery battery under Colonel Richard Gridley. A contemporary account of the battle articulated the nature of the mission as "the detachment, under the command of Colonel William Prescott of Pepperell, who had orders in writing from General Ward, was to proceed to Bunker Hill, build fortifications there, and defend them until he should be relieved, the order not to be communicated to the men until the detachment had passed Charlestown Neck. It was understood that reinforcements and refreshments be sent to Colonel Prescott the next morning."

Once Reverend Samuel Langdon had given spiritual comfort to the men, the detachment of about 940 men formed in marching order in the deepening twilight of Friday, June 16, and started to march eastward toward Charlestown Neck. Colonel Prescott, dressed in a new blue coat that served as a uniform, led the long column down the road followed by two sergeants carrying hooded lanterns that allowed light only to the rear to guide the men in the gathering darkness. Prescott was accompanied by Colonel Richard Gridley who had been one of the few provincials rewarded with a Regular commission in the British army for his service in the French and Indian War and had been on His Majesty's list of half-pay recipients until he was requested by his fellow colonials to join the Massachusetts army. Gridley served in the somewhat unusual dual capacity of chief of artillery and chief engineer and had badgered the Provincial Congress into paying him the rather huge sum of £170 per year plus a guarantee of £123 per year for the rest of his life which made him the highest paid colonel in the army. Gridley was a competent engineer, but at age 65 he tired easily, was a difficult man to work with and had already used his position to obtain a captain's commission and a major's appointment for his two sons despite their lack of experience and training.

The provincial column marched in darkness through a series of orchards and streams near Lechmere Point, site of the British landing in the Concord expedition, and then entered a valley that separated Prospect Hill from Cobble Hill adjacent to Inman's Farm which served as headquarters for General Israel Putnam's Connecticut brigade. When Prescott reached the farm, he was joined by Knowlton's detachment of 200 men and by Putnam himself. The newly reinforced column of about 1,140 men then advanced to a major crossroads where one highway led to Winter Hill and the town of Medford while the other road led directly to Charlestown and its vital high ground. At this point the column commander explained his orders from General Ward to the men and the task force stumbled its way over the neck and onto the peninsula just about as the clocks in Boston were chiming 11 P.M.

Charlestown Peninsula, like Boston, was a virtual island connected to the mainland by a narrow neck that could go under water in unusually high tides or severe storms. The tip of the peninsula featured the town of Charlestown which included about 250 houses, a few stores and a handful of public buildings but had been almost totally abandoned in the aftermath of the brief British occupation of Bunker Hill after the retreat from Concord. The now empty town was separated from Boston by the 550-yard expanse of the Charles River which also flowed up the western side of the peninsula and backed up into a large bay, the end of which had been transformed into a millpond by the construction of a stone and piling dam about a quarter mile below the Neck. The eastern side of the peninsula featured the half-mile wide Mystic River which paralled the shoreline up from Moulton's Point which was the junction of the two rivers. The dominant topographical feature of the peninsula was a series of three hills, each one significantly larger than the next one to its south. Morton's Hill, 35 feet high, dominated the southeast corner of the pen-

Charlestown Peninsula—as seen from Boston—in 1775. The relative heights of Bunker Hill (1), Breed's Hill (2) and Moulton's Hill (3) are clearly shown. The causeway (4) and Charlestown (5) can also be seen.

insula and was so close to the tip of the peninsula that this prominence was only 600 yards away from the nearest British guns in Boston. The largest hill, on the northern end of the peninsula, was 110 feet high and called Bunker Hill. This height was a 300-yard-long oval running northwest to southeast that sloped down toward the Mystic River. In between these two points was a third hill which was connected to Bunker Hill by a low, sloping ridge and was 70 feet high at its peak elevation. Some local residents merely saw this middle hill as an appendage of Bunker Hill and referred to the prominence by the same name, but other citizens called this spot Charlestown Hill, Breed's Hill or by any of the names of owners of pasture and grazing land in the immediate vicinity. Thus when General Ward instructed Colonel Prescott to "secure and fortify Bunker Hill," there was plenty of room for a variety of interpretations as to just what constituted the real "Bunker Hill."

When the bulk of the slightly more than 1,100 patriots had crossed over Charlestown Neck, Prescott ordered the column to halt and began to confer with Colonel Gridley and General Putnam concerning the next appropriate move for the colonials. The three senior officers reconnoitered the darkened surroundings as best they could and then began to argue over which hill should actually be fortified. Colonel Gridley insisted that Bunker Hill was the only logical spot to fortify as it contained the highest elevation on the peninsula and already included a number of earthworks that had been constructed by British troops on the evening of the retreat from Concord. The British Redan, if properly extended and equipped with the four available rebel cannon, could dominate the Mystic River and all of the local roads. Also, the Neck was not accessible to the Regulars by water from the Charles River side because of the millpond while Bunker Hill itself was beyond the range and elevation of British naval guns. Thus the American position would be nearly impregnable and the British would have no opportunity to roll up the colonial lines and capture the vital stores at Cambridge.

While Colonel Gridley offered Prescott a series of coherent, rational arguments for fortifying Bunker Hill, Israel Putnam approached the dilemma far more emotionally. The Connecticut brigade commander insisted that Bunker Hill's distance from the British lines was also its greatest drawback as a fortification site. Putnam insisted that if the redcoat generals awoke the next morning to see rebel troops deployed on Bunker Hill, they would not perceive the position as an immediate threat and would merely shift the axis of their attack toward General Thomas' undermanned lines on the right flank at Roxbury. Thus Bunker Hill might very well close the front door to British attack, but would actually encourage the redcoats to smash into the poorly defended back door near Boston Neck and allow the Regulars to capture Cambridge from another direction. The Connecticut general argued that fortifying Breed's Hill would be far more effective because it would be much more likely to be perceived by the enemy as a threat to their army and their shipping and a goad to British pride that would almost force them to throw their main force into a costly attempt to capture the hill while leaving the Roxbury front as a sideshow. Putnam was convinced that the superior marksmanship of provincial fighting men would turn a redcoat assault on Breed's Hill into a first class British disaster that might well secure the liberties that Americans were fighting for in a single battle.

William Prescott was in a fairly unusual command position and he spent some time wavering between the two officers' arguments. Putnam was a superior officer but was a general in the army of another colony, and held direct command only over Captain Knowlton's 200-man detachment. However, he was already a legendary figure in American military history and his appeal to virtually force a battle of annihilation on the British probably stirred Prescott's emotions. On the other hand, Gridley was a professional engineer who was being paid an enormous salary to make the correct decisions on matters of fortification and he insisted that only Bunker Hill was a logical spot for the colonial forces to defend. Since many local residents considered Breed's Hill to be merely a spur of Bunker Hill anyway, Ward's orders could be liberally interpreted to mean either, or both, elevations. Ultimately Prescott decided to compromise but very much in Putnam's favor. Colonial troops would be deployed along Bunker Hill, but this position would serve primarily as a fallback point in case of an overwhelming British assault on the main American position to be fortified–Breed's Hill.

The series of reconnaisances, discussions, arguments and decision making among the American leaders took nearly an hour, and it was almost midnight before the provincials were implementing Prescott's operational plan. First, a company of men from Prescott's own regiment under Captain Robert Maxwell was ordered to patrol the shore in the lower part of the town, near the ferry terminal, and watch the activities of the British during the night. While Maxwell supervised the deployment of sentries, the rest of the men settled down in the town's meetinghouse and waited for dawn. A few hundred yards away, on the other side of the river, British sentries patrolled their lines with no hint of the activity opposite them. While Maxwell's men set up their screening positions, Gridley began staking out the outlines of a fort that would be 136 feet on each side: a box-shaped structure near the back of a plateau on Breed's Hill in an open, sloping meadow near the hill's highest peak. One corner pointed toward the Neck and one toward Boston so that the defenders would have a clear field of fire across the length and breadth of the hill on the two sides most susceptible to attack. The front of the redoubt, featuring a center in the arrow shape of a Redan faced the town of Charlestown and protected the south slope of Breed's Hill; the eastern side commanded the sloping meadows and the approach from the Charles River. The north side was constructed to allow a narrow entrance that could also be used to evacuate the fort if the defenders were in danger of being overwhelmed. Gridley's construction plan was well thought out, but he absent-mindedly forgot to make allowances for either gun platforms or embrasures through which the small number of rebel cannon could be fired. As the church clocks in Boston began to strike midnight, the provincial soldiers were issued picks and shovels and ordered to begin constructing the Breed's Hill redoubt. Since much of the success of the operation depended on keeping the British troops ignorant of what was happening on Charlestown Peninsula until at least sunrise, no one talked and the digging was kept as quiet as possible. A short distance away, four British ships, *Lively, Falcon, Symmetry* and *Glasgow,* mounting a total of 78 guns, rolled quietly at anchor while the muffled sounds of spades continued in the darkness.

Colonel Prescott was deeply concerned that the watch aboard the British ships would hear the rebels digging and he and Major John Brooks made several trips down to the edge of the Charles River to detect any sign of enemy alarm. Prescott had already determined that he would not be taken alive if his men could not stop a redcoat assault. A few months earlier, when his Loyalist brother-in-law tried to dissaude him from taking command of a provincial militia regiment with hints that such a move could result in hanging, Prescott replied, "I think it probable I may be found in arms, but I will never be taken alive. The Tories shall never have the satisfaction of seeing me hanged." However, while Prescott had already made up his mind never to allow himself to be captured alive, the Regular cry of "all's well" on each of the British warships provided the rebel commander with hope that his men would have enough time to construct a fortification that might very well annihilate a redcoat assault force.

Perhaps the first British Regular who became aware of the American activities that evening was Sir Henry Clinton. The British general had been out reconnoitering on this warm early summer night and he apparently heard the colonials at work on Charlestown Peninsula. Sir Henry hurried back to Province House, woke General Gage, and urged him to rouse the army for a dawn attack. According to Clinton, Gage "seemed to doubt the rebels' intentions" and decided to do nothing until daylight revealed the extent of the provincials' activities. Clinton returned dejectedly to his quarters and penned a letter to a friend in England that summarized his opinion of his commanding general. "If we were of active dispositions, we should be landed by tomorrow morning at daybreak, as it is, I fear it must be deferred until at least two o'clock in the afternoon."

Gage's failure to respond to Clinton's warning gave the patriot detachment almost five precious hours to construct fortifications with no interference from the enemy. However, when the sun rose at 4:35 A.M. on an already sultry Saturday morning, British quiescence ended very rapidly. A lookout aboard H.M.S. *Lively* was the first Englishman to actually see the result of rebel activities when he spotted a line of entrenchments traced across the green background of the middle hill on Charlestown Peninsula. When the lookout reported this incredible sighting to the ship's master, Thomas Bishop, the British captain put a spring on *Lively*'s cable and opened fire on the provincial works. Almost as soon as the guns broke the calm of the early morning sunrise, Bishop also dispatched an adjutant to Admiral Graves requesting further orders. The incompetent, corrupt British naval commander, awakened from a deep sleep at such an early hour, promptly sent a blistering message back to his captain ordering a cease-fire and censuring his decision to open fire without orders from the admiral. For a brief time the colonial troops were able to resume work without interference, but when General Gage received reports of Graves' orders he quickly countermanded the naval commander and ordered all British guns in effective positions to bombard the American entrenchments.

The onset of full daylight conditions encouraged a sobering appraisal of their positions on the part of both Colonel Prescott and General Gage. Prescott was highly pleased at the progress of his men in their fortification activities and he believed that the new redoubt was well constructed. However, daylight also revealed that Breed's Hill was vulnerable to a flank attack from two directions. The British commander could

Colonists fortifying Breed's Hill. This remarkable feat of military engineering by civilians, accomplished in a single night, took the British completely by surprise.

either ferry troops over from Boston and march along the bank of the Mystic River to strike the redoubt from behind, or push a large force of redcoats through the streets of Charlestown and bottle up the colonials from the opposite side of the hill. Many of Prescott's men were able to see the potential danger to their position. As one private later noted, "we saw our danger, being against eight ships of the line and all Boston fortified against us; the danger we were in made us think there was treachery and that we were brought there to be all slain; I must and will venture to say that there *was* treachery, oversight or presumption in the conduct of our officers." This feeling of unease began to intensify when the first casualty was suffered among the colonials. While the defenders were generally well-protected against British cannons by deep ditches and well-constructed parapets, one unfortunate militiaman, Asa Pollard of Billerica, was decapitated by a cannonball and his particularly gory death shocked dozens of his fellow soldiers. Prescott refused a chaplain's request to hold services for the dead colonial and then, to inspire confidence in his shaken troops, climbed on top of a parapet and calmly walked around the whole fortification, carefully inspecting each element of the redoubt as British cannonballs whizzed by.

Spectators in Boston could clearly see the tall provincial officer outlined against the sky and patriot sympathizers cheered the courage of the blue-coated colonel. One of the spectators was General Gage, who had just climbed to the steeple of Christ Church and was viewing the American fortification through a telescope. Gage turned to one of his Loyalist militia commanders, Colonel Josiah Willard, handed him the glass and asked if he recognized the prominent rebel commander. Willard, a member of the Governor's Council and a leading Boston Tory, immediately nodded in recognition and informed the British commander that the rebel was his brother-in-law, William Prescott. Gage inquired about Prescott's military background and asked the Council member if his relative would actually fight if the British landed an assault force. Willard replied, "Yes sir, he is an old soldier and will fight as long as a drop of blood remains in his veins." Gage took a final look at his rebel opponent and issued a terse order to his subordinates on the scene: "The works must be carried."

On the other side of the Charles River, Prescott was attempting to stiffen the weakening resolve of his men. Oppressive heat, exhausting construction work and a meager availability of food and drink produced a growing discontent among the soldiers and pleas from officers for Prescott to send a request to General Ward to order the dispatch of a replacement garrison. The provincial colonel offered a dramatic rebuttal to their pleas. "The enemy will not dare attack us and even if they do, they will be defeated; the men who have raised the works are the best able to defend them, already they have learned to despise the fire of the enemy, they had the merit of the labor and should have the honor of victory." While Prescott refused to request the replacement of the men, he did agree to send a high-ranking officer to Ward to ask for reinforcements and provisions. Major Brooks was delegated to return to colonial headquarters to secure additional men and supplies but when the major asked Colonel Gridley for the loan of an artillery horse, the only type of mount available, the chief engineer refused and Brooks began a four-mile hike to Cambridge while the animals that could have expedited his journey stood around unused on the meadows of Charlestown Peninsula.

While Brooks was trudging to Ward's headquarters, General Gage was assembling his senior officers at Province House for a critical council of war. The most adamant speaker was Sir Henry Clinton, who insisted that the rebels had obligingly provided His Majesty's army with a golden oportunity to crush the colonial rebellion. Sir Henry emphasized that Breed's Hill appeared to be undefended from the rear as the foolhardy

Sir Henry Clinton shortly before his actions at Bunker Hill. As in many drawings of the time, he is shown in the pre-1768 uniform, perhaps because Americans were familiar with it from the French and Indian War.

colonials "have put themselves in a bag and all we have to do is squeeze it." The former resident of New York proposed that a British landing force of 500 men should use the guns of the fleet for cover and seize the narrow neck that separated Charlestown Peninsula from the mainland. This would cut off either retreat or reinforcement for the rebels and the defenders would be forced to surrender or starve. If the provincials attempted to break out of the trap or if the rest of the colonial army tried to reinforce them, the guns of the fleet would annihilate them. Clinton also suggested that if Gage was uncomfortable with the prospect of waiting for the colonials to surrender, he could use the landing force to seize the unprotected enemy rear, employ the armed transport *Symmetry* and several floating batteries to overwhelm any rebel artillery fire, and deploy an additional assault force to hit the redoubt from the front while the initial detachment cut off the Americans' escape.

Clinton was confident that the British had both the trained forces and the firepower to annihilate the enemy defenders, but he insisted that the key ingredient to success was speed. An immediate attack would catch the rebels before they were totally ready to defend themselves as "at this moment, the rebel fort is incomplete, no flanks, neither picketed, palisaded or ditched," just an isolated outpost that could be gobbled up in a well-planned British pincers attack. Sir Henry's plan received the enthusiastic support of Colonel Timothy Ruggles, commander of Boston's Loyalist militia, who insisted that any delay in responding to the rapidly expanding rebel foothold on Charlestown Peninsula would mean the annihilation of an unsupported frontal assault by the Regulars. Ruggles proved to be Clinton's only supporter as Burgoyne and Howe vehemently opposed their colleagues' proposal and insisted that, because Sir Henry had never led an amphibious attack, he had not considered the numerous dangers of this type of operation. The two generals emphasized that Clinton's plan would break a cardinal principle of warfare by placing a smaller British force between two larger rebel armies, especially dangerous if the provincials were hiding large numbers of men on the far side of Bunker Hill. Howe insisted that British ships moving up the Mystic River to support an amphibious landing would be sailing in water that might be too shallow for safety while the landing force might become mired in a stretch of mud flats and flounder ashore with wet powder and useless weapons. Sir William also convinced Gage that from a political point of view the most substantial benefit from a British offensive must be the clear-cut ability of His Majesty's Regulars to meet and defeat the rebels on a battlefield of their own choosing. The reputation of the British army had been tarnished in the retreat from Concord, and could only be fully restored by thrashing the Americans on an open battlefield.

These arguments won the day for Burgoyne and Howe, and Gage politely dismissed Clinton's plan while seeking particulars from the other two generals on crushing the rebels in one blow. Howe responded confidently, "The hill is open and of easy ascent and in short, should be easily carried." British Regulars had covered themselves in glory in frontal assaults in Europe against professional adversaries; poorly trained "country people" should melt away before redcoat bayonets. Sir William may have admired the Americans as a people, but he was convinced that the colonists would not stand and fight in a conventional battle; thus one good application of British steel should remove the blot of Concord from the annals of His Majesty's forces.

Howe's enthusiasm for a frontal assault on Breed's Hill has often been criticized by both British and American historians as a microcosm of the unimaginative mindset of British officers in the War of Independence. However, it is readily apparent that Sir William had no intention of simply marching his men up a steep hill with the hope that a few would survive long enough to drive out the rebel defenders. Howe's plan was much more sophisticated and comprehensive and contained a number of elements that were expected to divert much of the rebel musket fire away from the main assault force. The basic operational plan was that a British landing force would disembark on the beach below the American redoubt where the guns of the fleet could smash any rebel attempt to sortie and drive the redcoats back into the river. A flying column of light infantry would rush up the Mystic River beach, knife across the American line of retreat and open fire on the redoubt from the rear. Once the colonials were fully engaged from the rear, the *Symmetry*, which could operate in shallow water, would move close to shore and provide naval fire support while Royal Artillery heavy guns emplaced in Copp's Hill would blast the redoubt with huge 24-pounders. Then, as the main assault force advanced, batteries of highly mobile 6-pounders would be wheeled into position behind the infantry and keep the rebels' heads down while the foot soldiers closed in on the fortifications. The result would be a rout of the demoralized defenders which would in turn serve as a springboard for a major push toward Cambridge where the rebel supply depots, and possibly most of the rebel army, would be captured by the Regulars before nightfall.

Gage warmly approved of his subordinates' plan and or-

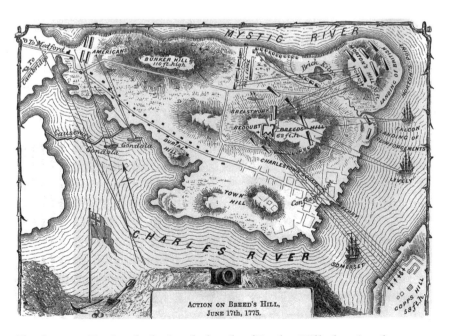

Charlestown Peninsula during the battle of Bunker Hill, showing the British fields of fire. The eastern tip, Moulton's Point, appears as Morton's Point in some maps and accounts of the time.

ders went out from Province House to almost every unit in the British garrison to prepare for their roles in the coming offensive. Ten companies of light infantry, ten companies of grenadiers and the battalion companies of the 5th and 38th regiments of foot were ordered to draw ammunition, provisions and blankets and march by files to Long Wharf in preparation for embarkation as the first assault wave. The 43rd and 52nd regiments of foot along with four companies of light infantry and four companies of grenadiers were instructed to march to North Battery which would be their debarkation point. The 47th Regiment of Foot and the 1st Battalion of Royal Marines were directed to assemble and move out to the same location after the first two regiments had been ferried across the Charles River to Charlestown. All other troops in the garrison, beyond a skeleton force assigned to guard the camps, were ordered to hold themselves in readiness to march at a moment's notice in order to exploit the expected initial success of the assault force. The initial operation would be carried out by 2,200 infantry and 100 artillerymen, a force just about twice the size of the 1,140 men that Prescott had led onto Charlestown Peninsula a few hours earlier. Actually, the odds favoring the British forces were improving steadily because during the course of the early morning hours individuals, platoons and even entire companies of rebels had gradually drifted back from the American entrenchments to either await developments in the comparative safety of Bunker Hill or the even more secure territory on the far side of Charlestown Neck. By late morning, something less than 600 provincial soldiers were actually deployed in the main line of colonial defense with almost four times that number of redcoats preparing to attack them.

Although almost half of his original detachment had drifted away from the defenses on Breed's Hill, Colonel Prescott was determined to deploy his remaining men to maximum advantage to destroy the British assault force. The colonial commander had already felt somewhat more optimistic when Israel Putnam agreed to ride back to Cambridge and badger Artemus Ward into sending substantial reinforcements. Meanwhile, Prescott ordered his available men to begin constructing a breastwork on the left side of the redoubt in order to extend the colonial defenses closer to the Mystic River shoreline. While his men worked on this 150-yard extension of the American defenses, the colonel anxiously studied the road leading to the Neck for some tangible evidence that either Brooks or Putnam had secured additional men.

Israel Putnam's access to a horse enabled the Connecticut general to arrive in Cambridge ahead of the Massachusetts major, and the famous veteran of the colonial wars was able to convince Ward to dispatch a New Hampshire regiment under John Stark to support Prescott. The American commanding general was still convinced it was a mistake to strip the main colonial lines to pour irreplaceable men into a potential death-trap, and by the time the dusty, overheated Brooks reported to headquarters Ward's reservations were mounting rapidly. The American general was also in agony from a major gall bladder attack, and when Brooks started relaying Prescott's request for substantial reinforcements, Ward simply threw up his hands and escorted the major into an emergency meeting of the Committee of Safety which was getting underway in an adjoining room. The chairman of the committee, Dr. Joseph Warren, was also writhing in pain from a blinding migraine headache and had already withdrawn to an upstairs bedroom when Brooks arrived. Therefore much of the responsibility for making one of the most critical decisions of the American Revolution fell on the shoulders of the committee's vice chairman, Richard Devens. Devens, unlike Ward, was emotionally committed to the idea of fighting the climactic battle on Charlestown Peninsula, and he readily agreed to start funneling significant elements of the colonial army toward Prescott's outnumbered defenders. Ward was directed to send several additional New Hampshire companies, and Colonel James Reed's Connecticut regiment to reinforce Prescott from their positions near Charlestown Neck while nine additional Massachusetts regiments would be marched from Cambridge to Charlestown as soon as they could be mobilized. The American commanding general was still convinced that the real British intention was to feint at Charlestown and then pour across Boston Neck to

Roxbury and roll up the colonial lines at Cambridge by sunset. Ironically, under the curious command arrangement of the provincial forces, Ward obeyed the orders of the Committee of Safety's temporary chairman to employ about half the rebel army, somewhere between 5,000 and 6,000 men, in a climactic battle against the redcoats in a position that Ward was convinced was the worst place to fight.

However, even though much of the colonial army was now committed, General William Howe's impressive assault force was already on its way to attack the outnumbered defenders of Charlestown Peninsula.

General Thomas Gage (1721-1787)

Thomas Gage was born in Firle, England, the second son of a relatively obscure noble family that remained Roman Catholic long after the Reformation. The Gage family included men who had backed King John against the nobles demanding his signature of Magna Carta, men who served as jailors of Princess Elizabeth when she was incarcerated by Queen Mary, and supporters of King James II when he was replaced by his daughter and son-in-law. Six years before Gage's birth, family fortunes had begun to improve when his grandfather, William Gage, converted to Protestantism, followed closely by his son's marriage to a wealthy heiress who quickly inherited an enormous fortune.

While Gage's parents were both high-living, outgoing individuals, Thomas Gage was serious, courteous and studious, and was considered to be an outstanding student at Westminster School. By the time Gage was 19 years old, his brother was an influential member of parliament and an initial commission as a lieutenant in the British army was followed by rapid promotions and choice assignments. After significant roles in campaigns against the French and the Scottish rebels, Gage was sent to America where he served as commander of Braddock's advance force in the expedition to Fort Duquesne. Gage was given significant credit for extricating the survivors of the ambush from certain annihilation even though it is likely that George Washington and his provincial troops were most responsible for saving the remnants of the column.

Gage utilized his wilderness experiences when he was given command of the 80th Regiment of Foot which he modeled on provincial ranger units with a strong emphasis on mobility and use of cover. However this unit was almost annihilated, and Gage himself seriously wounded, in an ill-advised frontal assault on French-held Fort Ticonderoga. Subsequent to Gage's recovery, he was promoted to brigadier general and given command of the British column that was expected to capture Montreal while Wolfe's expedition assaulted Quebec. While Wolfe secured Quebec, and died in the process, Gage's column was floundering through the wilderness and never reached its target. Despite this embarrassing failure, the new king, George III, took a personal interest in Gage and he was quickly promoted to major general and given command of all of His Majesty's forces in America at the end of the Seven Years War.

The new major general followed up his military advancement with a highly publicized marriage to a beautiful American heiress, Margaret Kemble of New Jersey, a member of one of the most powerful families in the colonies. By 1774 Gage held title to huge estates in New Jersey, upstate New York and the West Indies, and was one of the wealthiest lieutenant generals in the British army. On the other hand, a combination of baldness, a sickly skin coloration and a premature aging process made this powerful general still in the prime of his life look like a man about 20 years older than his actual age. After the battle of Bunker Hill, Gage was recalled to London for "consultation" with the government concerning future prosecution of the suppression of the rebellion, but by April 1776 he was formally dismissed as commander in chief of North America. However, George III was still friendly to the general and he was appointed chief of staff to General Jeffrey Amherst in 1781, and promoted to full general in 1782 with responsibility for directing the home defenses of England against an expected French invasion. Gage died at his home in Portland, England on April 2, 1787.

Sir Henry Clinton (1738-1795)

The initially most energetic and decisive of the three generals arriving in Boston on H.M.S. *Cerebus* was Sir Henry Clinton. Clinton was born in Newfoundland but grew up in New York where his father was royal governor. He served as a militia officer in a local unit until he returned to England to assume a commission in the Grenadier Guards. His influential cousin, the Duke of Newcastle, procured for him a lieutenant colonelcy at the age of 20 and his brilliant service in the Seven Years War led to a major generalship and a seat in parliament.

Sir Henry was viewed as a moderately pro-American member of the House of Commons, who was also deeply devoted to his wife and children and appalled by the corruption and loose morals of large numbers of British leaders. During the growing crisis with the colonies, Clinton insisted that he had no desire to accept a command in America. But after the unexpected death of his wife, Sir Henry agreed to an assignment in Massachusetts largely to divert his emotions from his personal grief. Upon his arrival in Boston, Clinton immediately urged Gage to seize Dorchester Heights and subsequently developed the audacious plan for an amphibious assault on the rear of the American position at Breed's Hill. At

this point in the war, Clinton was probably the most intelligent, capable general in the British Army but his reserved personality and inability to get along with other generals would plague him during the Boston Campaign and in subsequent commands.

After the British evacuation of Boston, Clinton presided over the disastrous assault on Charleston in the summer of 1776 and he returned to Britain prepared to resign his commission and concentrate on parliamentary activities. King George intervened and Sir Henry returned to America where he assumed command of British forces in the spring of 1778 on the resignation of William Howe. He engineered a spectacularly successful second assault on Charleston but then turned over operational command in the South to Lord Cornwallis while he returned to New York. Clinton made significant attempts to relieve the British garrison besieged at Yorktown, but was severely hampered by lack of naval cooperation. He was relieved as commander in chief in May of 1782 and criticized for his role in the British defeat on his return to England. However, the King promoted Clinton to full general and made him royal governor of Gibraltar where he served until his death in 1795.

Sir William Howe (1729-1814)

General William Howe was born in 1729, the third son of an Irish peer, Viscount Howe, and his wife Mary Sophia, who was the illegitimate daughter of King George I. Sir William was educated at Eton, and along with his brothers George Augustus and Richard, enjoyed a warm personal relationship with his kinsman, George III. At age 17 William Howe was commissioned in the Duke of Cumberland's light dragoons and by the outbreak of the Seven Years War commanded the 58th Regiment of Foot. Sir William distinguished himself under Wolfe at the siege of Louisbourg and was a brigade commander by the end of the war. Along with Thomas Gage, he attracted considerable attention when he demonstrated the offensive power of specially trained, light infantry units.

After the defeat of France, Howe was elected to his dead brother's parliamentary seat for Nottingham and consistently supported the rights of the colonists in their feud with the British ministry. In the winter of 1774 he assured his constituents that he would never accept a field command in America but changed his mind at the personal intervention of the king, who also promised Howe authority to negotiate a settlement to the conflict. North viewed Howe as the most logical successor to the discredited Gage as he was believed to possess an exceptional understanding of the peculiarities of warfare in North America.

Howe assumed command of the British army in America on Gage's departure on October 10, 1775, and then commanded the army units of a joint army-navy command with his brother, Admiral Richard Howe. After the evacuation of Boston, Sir William won every engagement with the Americans in which he was in direct field command, scoring significant victories at Long Island, Fort Washington and Brandywine, but his inability to adequately respond to Washington's thrusts at Trenton and Princeton and his failure to properly support Burgoyne's march toward Albany decisively damaged British prospects for victory and induced him to resign his command in May of 1778.

Following his return to England, Howe resumed his political career, held a number of important staff positions in the army and was eventually promoted to permanent rank of full general. He became an earl on the death of his brother Richard in 1799 and exercised significant influence on British strategy in the first stages of the war with Revolutionary France.

General John Burgoyne (1722-1792)

The oldest, but most militarily junior of the generals dispatched by the British government to support Thomas Gage was John Burgoyne. Born in Lancashire and educated at Westminster School, Burgoyne purchased a commission in the 13th Light Dragoons at the age of 18, transferring to the 1st Royal Dragoons four years later. In 1751 he stunned much of British society by eloping with Lady Charlotte Stanley, daughter of the powerful Earl of Derby. The earl disinherited his daughter and Burgoyne's enormous gambling debts forced him to sell his commission, resign from the army, and take ship for France to avoid his many creditors.

At the outbreak of the Seven Years War, Derby and his son-in-law were reconciled and the earl promptly secured him the colonelcy of the 16th Dragoons, known as "Burgoyne's Light Horse." In 1763 Burgoyne entered parliament as the member from Midhurst and began a successful career as a playwright while still retaining command of his regiment, that was now named "Queen Charlotte's Dragoon's" after King George's wife. By 1772 the cavalry officer had been promoted to major general and enjoyed a close relationship with George III, who considered Burgoyne one of his most talented generals and pressed Lord North to appoint him to a post in Massachusetts in February of 1775.

Burgoyne's role in the Boston campaign was the least active of the three generals who arrived on H.M.S. *Cerebus* as he did little more than observe the battle of Bunker Hill from the safety of Boston. Apparently he made a nuisance of himself when Howe assumed command, returning to England in the fall of 1775, spent only a brief interval in North America before going to Canada to assume command of the Hudson River expedition of 1777. Burgoyne was immediately paroled by Horatio Gates after the surrender at Saratoga and was ultimately made commander in chief of British forces in Ireland upon his return.

At the end of the War of Independence the general retired from active duty to devote himself to literary and social pursuits and died suddenly in London in 1792.

CHAPTER VII

The British Assault on Charlestown Peninsula

Shortly after noon on the sunny, hot afternoon of June 17, 1775, 28 Royal Navy barges pushed off from Long Wharf and North Battery and began to glide toward the far shore of the Charles River. The vessels were formed up into two parallel lines of 14 barges each and were loaded to capacity with redcoated British Regulars. Civilian spectators in Boston, British officers standing on top of Copp's Hill and the provincial troops manning the redoubt at Breed's Hill all took careful note of the drama and pageantry that accompanied this form of 18th-century warfare. Long oars swept back and forth across the third of a mile of blue water separating Boston and Charlestown. An eyewitness noted "the sun was shining in meridian splendor and the scarlet uniforms, the glistening armor, the brazen artillery, the flashes of fire and the belchings of smoke formed a spectacle brilliant and imposing."

As the barges began to close in on their landing beach at Moulton's Point, a barrage of navy and army cannon swept the shoreline. The *Falcon* and the *Lively* swept the low ground in front of Breed's Hill to dislodge any rebels that might be deployed to oppose the landing on the shore; *Somerset*, two floating batteries and the army battery on Copp's Hill poured solid shot on the American earthworks; *Glasgow* and *Symmetry* moved up the Charles River and began raking Charlestown Neck with heavy fire. About 30 minutes after the artillery barrage began, the first Regulars splashed ashore on the beach and deployed around Moulton's Point while the barges returned to Boston for their second detachment of troops. It was nearly three o'clock before the barges returned and disembarked the 47th Regiment of Foot and the 1st Battalion of Royal Marines at the Old Battery and Mardlin's shipyard further down the beach from the landing zone for the initial assault force. While the barges were undertaking their second ferrying operation, Howe conducted a careful reconnaissance of the rebel works. Sir William was particularly concerned that the colonials had added a new breastwork to cover the flank of the redoubt while other provincials seemed to be deploying behind fences that stretched toward the Mystic River. The British general decided to postpone the attack until further reinforcements could be embarked and while the barges returned to Boston for a third group of redcoats, the Regulars who had already landed were told to undo their knapsacks and eat lunch while Sir William updated his plan of attack.

The substantial delay in implementing the British assault gave Prescott and the newly returned Israel Putnam additional time to expand the American defense line. However, an integral part of the colonial formation began to unravel when the two artillery battery commanders, Captain Samuel Gridley and Captain John Callender, suddenly decided that their four guns could not be properly defended by the limited number of infantry available and arbitrarily began ordering their gunners to seize dragropes and pull the cannon back across Charlestown Neck. When General Putnam, who was supervising the digging of entrenchments on Bunker Hill, noticed the guns being pulled back from the American lines he confronted the two officers and demanded an explanation. The two artillery commanders sheepishly insisted that they were out of ammunition, but when Putnam checked the guns' side boxes he found full loads of cannonballs. The Connecticut general ordered the artillerymen to return the cannon to Breed's Hill, but when Putnam rushed off to manage several other crises, the gunners simply abandoned their pieces and crossed over to the mainland, leaving the entire American artillery arm standing in a meadow while more than 100 British cannon were bombarding the colonial defenses.

The evaporation of colonial artillery support was somewhat counterbalanced by a substantial strengthening of the primary American fortifications. The first provincial reinforcements began crossing over Charlestown Neck at about the same time that General Howe was reconnoitering the rebel positions and several units deployed rapidly to screen the vulnerable colonial left flank. James Reed's and John Stark's New Hampshire regiments were some of the first reinforcing units to arrive on the field, and the New Hampshire men quickly joined Captain Knowlton's Connecticut contingent in extending the American line beyond the newly constructed breastwork. Knowlton had already begun to deploy his 200 men in the first likely defensive position to the left of the main American fortifications, a series of rail fences which ran parallel to the new breastwork but were located about 200 yards closer to the Neck and were bounded on one side by a road leading up Bunker Hill and on the other by the bank of the Mystic River. The Connecticut men grounded arms near the main series of fences and then carried rails from less strategically located structures to strengthen the front line. As one of Knowlton's officers recounted "our position was behind a fence half of stone and half of wood. Here nature had formed something of a breastwork or else there had been a ditch many years ago." The colonials then stuffed hay between the rails to make the structure look much more solid than it really was, hoping to bluff the Regulars into believing they were confronting a position almost impervious to bullets.

The series of fences substantially extended the colonial defenses but there still remained considerable open space between Knowlton's left flank and the bank of the Mystic River in one direction, and between the Connecticut contingent's right flank and the rebel breastwork in the other direction. The Connecticut captain was able to solve part of this problem by ordering his men to dig three V-shaped trenches, called fleches, which filled in much of the gap on his right flank while the newly-arrived men from the Granite colony took care of the left. The New Hampshire units had arrived on the mainland side of Charlestown Neck as *Symmetry's* 18 9-pounders raked the narrow entry to the peninsula. Despite the pleas of his subordinates for speed, Stark boldly ordered his men to walk, not run, over the causeway as he insisted that exhausted men were worth far less than well-rested ones. The regiments made their way safely through the British barrage and Stark halted his men near Bunker Hill, delivered a "short but animated" address to the troops followed by three cheers and then began the deployment of his companies. Reed's regiment and part of Stark's contingent, under regimental adjutant Major Adam McClary, deployed behind a series of fences and walls that stretched from Knowlton's left flank to the edge of a cliff overlooking the Mystic River beach eight or nine feet below. Stark himself led several of his own companies in a scrambling descent down to the narrow shoreline. Stark took particular interest in this deployment because he was convinced that the most vulnerable point on the whole American line was the Mystic River beach. If Howe could march a force along the water's edge just below the cliffs, he could climb back up to the adjoining fields and meadows behind the rail fences and hit the colonials from behind. The New Hampshire colonel tersely ordered his men to haul stones from the cliffs down to the beach and a triple wall was constructed right to the water's edge and manned with the regiment's best sharpshooters.

By about 3 P.M. on this torrid Saturday afternoon, the American position was essentially complete with four distinct strongpoints in place. The main positions were the original redoubt on Breed's Hill, the breastwork adjacent to the redoubt, the line of rail fences to the river bank and the stone walls on the beach below. The arrival of several companies each from the Massachusetts regiments commanded by colonels Brewer, Bridge, Nixon, Woodbridge, Little and Moore gave Colonel Prescott elements of nine regiments, all from Massachusetts, to fortify the redoubt and the breastwork. The American position from the left end of the breastwork to the water's edge was held by Knowlton's contingent and the two New Hampshire regiments. The right flank of the American redoubt ended on a portion of Breed's Hill that was about 1,000 yards from the town of Charlestown and was primarily a sloping expanse that featured a narrow cart track etched through the grass. Prescott had assigned a single company to deploy along the cart track itself while three companies had been dispatched into the abandoned town to support Maxwell's small screening force. While these men had concealed themselves well among the town's empty buildings, there were only about 150 men deployed in Charlestown and they had access to little direct support from the main colonial garrison.

Twelve New England regiments were represented in the American front lines on this climactic afternoon but Colonel Prescott commanded very few full-strength units. While almost half of the men from the original three regiments had drifted back away from the redoubt, the reinforcing units had dribbled toward Charlestown Peninsula a company or two at a time. Some units were milling around Bunker Hill, some companies huddled near the Neck, and a large number of units were still assembling on the mainland at Charlestown Common when the British attack began. Thus the 5,000 or 6,000 men who were technically at Prescott's disposal were whittled to a small fraction of that number at the point of engagement that afternoon. The American field commander estimated that at the time of the British attack he could deploy about 150 men in the town, 150 men in the redoubt itself, 200 men in the new breastwork, and 400 men along the rail fences and down on the beach. Thus Prescott could count on about 900 men to confront a British assault force that had already landed 2,300 men and had another 500 Regulars preparing to cross the Charles River, while between four and five thousand additional colonial troops were in the vicinity of the battlefield but ultimately would take no part in the battle.

As the afternoon temperature soared toward 95 degrees and the British assault regiments began to stir from their meals, the tensions in the colonial lines reached even higher levels. As one contemporary participant noted, "by mid-afternoon intense anxiety prevailed in the entrenchments on Breed's Hill. The patriot band who raised them had witnessed the efficient landing of the British veterans and the return of the barges to Boston. They saw troops again filling the boats and felt not without apprehension that a battle was inevitable. They knew that the contest would be an unequal one, that of raw militia against hardened Regulars and they grew impatient for reinforcements. It is not strange, therefore, that the idea was entertained that they had been rashly if not treacherously, led into danger and that they were to be left to their own resources for their defense!" Only a trickle of additional reinforcements would reach the American lines before the redcoats struck, but among the handful of additional men were two well-known patriot celebrities, General Seth Pomeroy, hero of the French and Indian War, and Dr. Joseph Warren, chairman of the Committee of Safety and a newly-commissioned major general of militia. Both men briskly walked up the slope to the redoubt and, accompanied by the cheers of the defenders, took stations in the ranks as volunteers while assuring the men that aid was coming shortly. Warren insisted that 2,000 additional men would be arriving within 20 minutes while Israel Putnam rode down from his station on Bunker Hill to assure the front-line defenders that he had sent messengers to speed up the arrival of reinforcements from Cambridge.

The exhortations of the colonial leaders to the provincial soldiers had an equally emotional counterpart in the British lines. General Howe ordered the assault units assembled and when everyone was properly aligned, delivered the kind of address that had already made him popular among his men. Sir William insisted, "Gentlemen, I am very happy in having the honour of commanding so fine a body of men; I do not in the least doubt but that you will behave like Englishmen and as becomes good soldiers. If the enemy will not come out from their entrenchments, we must drive them out at all events, otherwise, the town of Boston will be set on fire by them. I shall not desire one of you to go a step further than where I go myself at your head." The British general then interjected a measure of the gravity of the situation when he admonished the

Regulars, "Remember, gentlemen, we have no recourse to any resources if we lose Boston but to go on board our ships which will be very disagreeable to us all." Then Sir William sent out strong flank guards and directed his field pieces to bombard the rebel lines to cover the infantry advance.

Howe had decided to launch the attack from two wings, a right flank under his personal command and a left flank under Brigadier General Robert Pigot. The British commander was convinced that the rebel left flank was their main weak point. Most of the troops on that flank had been observed deploying in the area only within the last hour or two and presumably had not had enough time to complete a formidable series of defenses. Sir William also assumed that the Americans had only deployed as far as the river bank, and felt there was no evidence the rebels had taken the precaution of defending the narrow beach front. Therefore, while Pigot's detachment demonstrated against the colonial redoubt, 10 companies of light infantry would march rapidly up the Mystic beach, climb up to the river bank well behind the front row of rail fences and smash the provincials from the rear. Meanwhile, 10 companies of grenadiers would form a shock force that would menace the defenders and distract their attention from the threat that was developing behind them. Once the grenadiers and light infantry caught the colonials in a pincers, the battalion companies of the 5th and 57th regiments would rush forward to add their bayonets and numbers to the engagement which, if all went well, would be developing into a rout by this stage of the battle.

Once the 36 companies under Howe's direct command had fully engaged the eastern wing of the rebel defense line, General Pigot's 38 companies would turn their demonstration attack into the real thing. This imposing force of three companies of light infantry, three companies of grenadiers, the battalion companies of the 38th, 43rd and 47th regiments and the Royal Marine battalion would skirt around the abandoned buildings of Charlestown, move around the fringe of Breed's Hill and strike the rebel redoubt from the side. Pigot had already determined to carry the works by bayonet alone, depending on the support of a battery of 6-pounders to keep the rebels' heads down during the final sprint to the colonial entrenchments. Howe and Pigot had developed an intelligent, sophisticated assault plan that could produce an overwhelming British victory if everything went roughly according to their projections. However, piece by piece, this carefully developed strategy began to unravel in the afternoon heat.

At just past three o'clock on Saturday afternoon, June 17, long lines of British infantry began to step off while a pair of 12-pounders on Moulton's Point boomed their support. However, as Royal Artillery gunners wheeled their mobile 6-pounders into position behind the advancing infantry, the battery commander realized to his horror that the guns' side boxes were filled with 12-pound cannon balls. Colonel Samuel Cleaveland, Gage's chief of artillery, was recognized as one of the most incompetent, corrupt officers in the British high command, and the artillery commander had apparently supplied the wrong ammunition to the batteries while he was preoccupied with conducting romantic affairs with two of the daughters of one of the most prominent Loyalists in Boston. Howe considered the mobile artillery support to be one of the keys to a successful assault and now, until additional ammunition could be ferried over from Boston, the redcoats would have to attack without vital suppressing fire.

The second factor that caused Sir William's plan to unravel was the general's conviction that the colonials would not bother to fortify the narrow Mystic River beach which in turn would allow his light infantry companies to push up the narrow strand largely unopposed. However, the beach was now anything but an open route to the colonial rear as Colonel Stark's men had just finished erecting stone barriers to bar the redcoats. When the improvised walls were finished, Stark sprang over the most forward fortification and hammered a stake into the sand 40 yards in front of the defenders. The New Hampshire commander then ordered, "not a man is to fire until the first Regular crosses that stake; watch their gaiters. When you can see their gaiters clear, that's when to shoot." In essence, Stark was ordering his marksmen to aim low so that the

John Stark in general's uniform later in the Revolutionary War. Although already 48 at the time of Bunker Hill, he outlived all the other generals of the Revolution.

recoil of their guns would send the bullets into the redcoats' chests.

As the long column of light infantrymen rounded a curve of the beach and the first stone wall came into view, the redcoats began to realize that Howe's insistence that the shoreline would not be defended was in error. However, the rebel fortification seemed to be little more than a knee-high pile of stones covering an undetermined number of rebels crouched behind the rocks. The light infantrymen were then ordered to prepare for a bayonet assault to sweep the colonials off the beach with cold steel. Each company was ordered to shift from marching order to attack formation and spread out in lines as wide as the narrow beach would permit. The Mystic beach was just wide enough to allow about 15 men to stand abreast of one another, so the 10 companies were able to form about 20 ranks deep on a front that was too narrow to permit the awesome weight of a British bayonet assault to be fully implemented. The captain of the lead company, the light infantry of the Welsh Fusiliers, gave the order for his two ranks to advance toward the stone wall. Just as the front line reached Stark's marker, the New Hampshire colonel lowered his arm in a dramatic gesture and a wall of flame erupted from the American position. The first volley killed or wounded over half of the fusiliers but the survivors continued to charge toward the stone wall. A second rebel volley virtually annihilated the company as five or six dazed survivors watched their comrades fall onto the beach. Almost as the Welshmen were dropping to the sand, another company, the light infantry from the King's Own Regiment moved over the dead and wounded fusiliers and leveled their bayonets for a charge. The men of this 4th Regiment of Foot assumed that the colonials must be reloading their weapons after firing two volleys and their captain was convinced that they could sprint over the stone wall and skewer the provincials before they could fire again. Unfortunately for the redcoats, Stark had hidden more men behind the wall than the British officers could notice and he ordered part of the force to hold their fire until the initial marksmen had fired. The King's Own men covered less than half the remaining distance to the wall when another sheet of flame erupted and dozens of elite troops crumpled with wounds. They lost perhaps 30 of their 35 men in less than a minute. Almost simultaneously, a third company of redcoats surged forward, the light infantry of the 10th Regiment who had torn through Captain Parker's men on Lexington Green two months earlier. The men closed to within perhaps 10 yards of the stone wall when yet another rank of concealed rebels suddenly popped up and sent another deadly volley smashing into the king's troops. Almost every member of this company was dead or wounded a few seconds later and the pitiful few survivors joined their fortunate few comrades of the first two companies in a dazed fallback.

Three of the most elite units in Gage's army had been annihilated in less than five minutes, but seven companies deploying over 200 men were still intact and their commanders were convinced they could overwhelm the colonials. These officers simply could not comprehend Stark's tactics of rotating ranks of men firing and loading so that an almost continuous fire could be maintained. As the remaining British companies surged forward, the New Hampshire colonel set up a rotation of three ranks and prepared to receive another bayonet charge. The most forward company of redcoats was that of the 52nd Regiment and these men advanced much more reluctantly as the shock of the carnage began to take effect. Officers had to shout and prod them into motion and when the Regulars passed Stark's marker stake, their fate was much the same as their predecessors. Dozens of men spun around and fell as surviving officers smashed at those men still standing with their swords. Elements of six other companies passed through the survivors and attempted a mass bayonet attack which began to evaporate half way to the stone wall. The sheer crush of each succeeding unit propelled the assault for a few brief minutes until the rebel volleys struck so many redcoats that an almost continuous carpet of fallen men halted any pretense of advance. By the time that surviving officers began shouting orders to retreat, much of the assault force had already turned and fled back down the beach toward Moulton's Point and safety. Dozens of their comrades were left dead or gravely wounded on the narrow beach. In a period of perhaps five to ten minutes, a staggering 96 light infantrymen had been killed and several dozen more redcoats seriously injured. One company had no surviving member above the rank of private and at least four companies had effectively been annihilated with 80 percent casualties. As Colonel Stark surveyed the results of his continuous volley fire he remarked "I never saw sheep lie as thick in the fold."

While the rear segment of Howe's planned pincers was evaporating, up on the grassy plateau that ended at the river bank, a double line of redcoats stretched halfway across the peninsula was marching forward in the sweltering heat. Ten companies of His Majesty's grenadiers lurched ahead slowly, burdened with knapsacks filled with three days' rations, blankets, cartridge boxes and other assorted impediments that multiplied their discomfort in the sweltering heat and humid-

British troops advance on the American positions. Although stylized, the print shows each company with its commander at the right of the line, accompanied by his drummer for signaling.

ity. Since most of the grass had not been mown since the battle of Concord, the Regulars marched through some sections of meadow that were waist high and concealed rocks and pot-holes. The sweating, grunting redcoats climbed over more than a dozen stone walls and rail fences, splashed through six or seven swampy bogs and tried to maneuver around an abandoned brick kiln, which threatened to disrupt the alignment that was so important to advancing armies in 18th-century warfare. Portions of the line stopped to climb over the impediments and then were forced to halt again a few minutes later to allow the next unit on their flank to catch up after scaling a different set of obstacles. Civilian spectators and British officers watching the advance from high ground in Boston remarked on the slow progress of the crimson line while colonials resting their muskets on the rail fences waited patiently for their adversaries to close in to better firing range. General Burgoyne, watching the unfolding panorama from the top of Copp's Hill, noted, "it was one of the greatest scenes of war that can be conceived; if we look to the height, Howe's corps ascending the hill in the face of entrenchments and in a very disadvantageous ground, was much engaged; to the left, the enemy pouring in fresh troops by the thousands, over the land [neck]; and in the arms of the sea, our ships and floating batteries cannonading them . . . the hills round the country covered with spectators, the enemy all in anxious suspense, and the reflection that, perhaps, a defeat was a final loss to the British Empire in America made the whole picture a combination of horror and importance beyond anything that ever came to my lot to be witness to."

As the grenadiers' approach to the colonial lines became more impeded by fences and walls, exasperated officers finally gave orders to their men to smash the rails with their musket butts and knock apart the piles of stones that were playing havoc with the Regulars' alignment. While Howe and his aides were encouraging their men to move more quickly, an ashen faced messenger came running up to Sir William and reported the annihilation of the flying column of light infantry down on the Mystic beach. Despite the shocking twin blows of losing his artillery support because of the wrong ammunition and losing his threat to the enemy rear because of Stark's brilliant improvisation, Howe outwardly maintained his calm demeanor and responded by ordering: "Attack all along the line." The British assault would now rise or fall on the bravery of professional soldiers charging directly toward a well-entrenched enemy.

The colonial troops manning the rail fences and walls on the left flank of the American line were standing in the same torrid sunlight as their adversaries, but they enjoyed two enormous advantages over their redcoated enemies. First, instead of being burdened with the choking stocks, oven-like wool coats and impractical bearskin hats of grenadiers, the colonials' attire of broad-brimmed hats and loose linen shirts free of knapsacks and other impediments allowed a degree of comfort and mobility denied to the advancing Regulars. Second, while the British troops had to exhaust themselves marching uphill through numerous barriers in the sweltering heat, the defenders could conserve their energy and rest on fence rails until their adversaries marched into range.

At least one man on the colonial left flank was not waiting passively for the redcoats to march into musket range. Israel Putnam had spotted Gridley's artillery battery soon after it was abandoned by its gunners, and the Connecticut general quickly ordered Captain John Ford's company to tow two of the guns into the 100-yard gap between the rail fence and the newly built breastwork. Ironically, Putnam discovered that Captain Callender might not have been able to use the pieces even if he had remained on the field as, similar to Howe's guns, the sideboxes were filled with the wrong ammunition. However, the problem with the American ammunition was not the size of the cannon balls but the powder bags, and Putnam simply slit a bag open, dumped the powder down the barrel with a ladle, rammed home a ball and then nearly blew himself to bits when he threw a match into the touch-hole since no safer linstock igniters were available. Putnam remained in one piece, and the first ball whistled over the heads of the advancing Regulars and landed in Boston Harbor. When the British Regulars were seen to be ignoring the small scale American artillery "bombardment," Putnam attempted to fire another round without cleaning out the barrel and the gun split down the side, cutting the rebel artillery force by 25 percent. However, the French and Indian War hero immediately rushed to his saddle bags, extracted perhaps 300 musket balls from their pockets and dumped the balls down the second cannon's barrel. When the British line advanced to the brick kilns, about 200 yards from the American rail fence, Putnam shoved a match into his cannon's touch-hole and a hail of canister-like balls tore through the scarlet ranks like a giant shotgun blast. Putnam now realized the deadly effect several well-placed American artillery batteries might have had on the advancing Regulars, but he also realized that he was needed more urgently in a command position. The general rounded up two provincials who volunteered to attempt to fire the gun and informed their commander that they knew of a British deserter who had joined their regiment and might be of some

Israel Putnam in the uniform he wore during the French and Indian War.

use. The former redcoat, Private Hill, did have some experience in the Royal Artillery and soon the two Americans and one Englishman were sending cannon balls ripping through the ranks of the oncoming Regulars. Unfortunately, after a few more rounds crashed into the redcoat lines, this second gun was also damaged from improper cleaning and, for the moment, American artillery support came to an abrupt end.

When the second colonial field piece was put out of action, General Howe and his grenadiers had cut the distance between themselves and the American defenders to less than 100 yards. At this point a number of the most confident New Hampshire sharpshooters opened fire on the advancing redcoats. Putnam screamed in rage at this threat to the shock of a massed volley fire and yelled, "I swear the next man who fires I'll take his head off." At about 70 yards' range the first Connecticut troops opened fire, this time prodded by their officers who wanted to entice the Regulars to fire back from maximum range and, hopefully, disrupt the alignment of their ranks. The tactic worked perfectly as the grenadiers halted to return fire while the trailing rank of battalion companies of the 5th and 52nd regiments of foot, caught by surprise, kept marching and crashed into the elite flank companies. Sir William quickly roared orders for the grenadiers to cease firing and form for a bayonet attack while Lt. Colonel James Abercromby raced up and down the lines aligning the men for their final rush to the enemy fences.

As the newly aligned grenadiers, perhaps 350 in number, lowered their muskets for a classic bayonet charge, the supporting guns on Moulton's Point and Copp's Hill fell silent for fear of hitting their own men on the final approach. The Regulars plodded through a last field of unmown hay, smashed their way through a final fence and halted just long enough to sweep forward in unison. At this point the redcoats were clearly within range of any American musket and Putnam yelled the single order "Fire!" to the Connecticut and New Hampshire defenders. A wall of flame belched out and the scarlet line simply evaporated. As one American participant noted, "many men were marksmen intent on cutting down the British officers and when one was in sight they exclaimed there! See that officer! Let us have a shot at him! And two or three would fire at the same moment." The eyewitness marveled at the accuracy of his companions as "they used the fence as a rest for their pieces and the bullets were true to their message. The companies were cut up with terrible severity and so great was the carnage that the columns, a few moments before so proud and firm in their array, were disconcerted, partly broke, and then retreated."

As the grenadiers began to disintegrate the battalion companies of the 5th and 52nd regiments were thrown in to solidify the British advance and for the next quarter of an hour these men tried to plunge forward through the heaps of dead and dying redcoats who had already gone down. One British officer remarked on the steady fire pouring from the rail fences and estimated that over 3,000 defenders were hidden behind the walls. "As we approached an incessant stream of fire poured from the rebel lines. Our men were served up in companies against the grass fence without being able to penetrate. Indeed, how could we penetrate? Most of our companies, at the moment of presenting themselves, lost three-fourths and many nine-tenths of their men."

Fifteen minutes after the redcoats came under colonial fire, the King's Own grenadier company had only four men standing, the Welsh Fusiliers counted only five men unwounded and the 52nd Grenadiers were down to eight survivors. Every officer and sergeant in the 10th Grenadiers was killed or wounded and Colonel Abercromby, a close friend of Putnam's from the French and Indian War days, was mortally wounded. General Howe survived the engagement but his personal staff took heavy casualties. His engineering officer went down with a shattered leg, his naval aide died with a bullet in his head, his personal aide toppled with a bullet in his chest and several other junior staff members were dead or dying. The grenadiers had suffered 80 percent casualties while the men of the 5th and 52nd regiments had lost well over half of their ranks. At this point Sir William was standing completely alone with a blood splattered uniform and every member of his entourage dead or seriously wounded around him. Screams of agony from wounded men replaced the earlier cheers and the screams so moved the colonials that one defender remarked 80 years later, at the age of 105, "it was louder than the firearms and I was pretty sick before I could pull a trigger again."

While Sir William Howe had personally witnessed the destruction of the detachment under his immediate command, he still hoped that his left wing under General Pigot had been able to overwhelm the rebels in the redoubt with their impressive array of infantry and marines. Pigot's men were advancing through smoky haze in the wake of one of Howe's most controversial decisions of his career. When the 38 companies of the British left wing had been assembling for their role in the grand assault, they came under heavy fire from the three companies of colonials deployed in the abandoned buildings of Charlestown who were acting as a screen for Prescott's garrison. A thoroughly annoyed and disgusted Howe fumed

Charlestown burns at the beginning of the Bunker Hill battle, the most controversial British action of the campaign.

at this sort of "unmanly" warfare and sent an aide to Admiral Graves requesting naval gunfire to rout the troublesome rebels from Charlestown. When Graves asked eagerly if his orders included the option of burning the town to the ground with incendiary ammunition, Sir William made no objection and a few minutes later Royal Navy vessels were pouring red-hot balls into Charlestown. Then a party of Royal Marines from H.M.S. *Somerset* sprinted into the eastern section of the town and set fire to buildings that hadn't been hit by the artillery barrage. Finally, the artillery stationed on the crest of Copp's Hill finished the razing of the town by firing carcass balls, filled with combustibles, into the already blazing community. One spectator in Boston noted with awe, "the eye was filled with the blaze of the burning town, fire coursing through whole streets or curling up the spires of public edifices, the air above filled with clouds of dense, black smoke."

The controversial burning of Charlestown might have driven the rebel sharpshooters from the main part of the town, but did not substantially aid Pigot's advance as the colonial marksmen simply retreated to a series of damaged buildings and kept dropping redcoats during their grudging withdrawal. The British wing commander was finally forced to divert most of his Royal Marines to flush out the rebel snipers in a deadly game of hide and seek which effectively reduced the force preparing to assault the main colonial redoubt by almost a quarter of the available troops.

Pigot directed his 38th and 43rd regiments to attack the eastern side of the fort while the 47th Regiment and a small force of remaining marines would strike the south side closest to Charlestown. Apparently the British brigadier was unsure whether this attack was primarily a demonstration in force intended to divert American attention from Howe's sphere of operations or actually supposed to be a full-fledged assault with the intention of carrying the enemy fortifications. One result of this confusion was a poorly coordinated operation in which the two separate assault forces managed to advance at two different times. Prescott quickly noticed the poor coordination of the enemy attacks and shrewdly shifted units to counter each assault in succession. Once American volleys had decimated the eastern assault force, Prescott rushed much of his force to the south wall and repeated the process all over again on the second group of advancing redcoats. Pigot suffered severe casualties, although not nearly the carnage facing Howe, and then pulled his men out of range on the assumption that a "demonstration attack" was all that Sir William really intended. The defenders of the redoubt, much like their comrades behind the rail fence and stone wall, looked out on dozens of redcoats sprawled in the grass and realized that the first round in the battle of Bunker Hill had clearly been a colonial victory.

General John Stark (1728-1822)

Stark was born in Londonderry, New Hampshire in 1728 and developed an interest in military affairs. He served as a captain in Rogers' Rangers during the French and Indian War and returned home to a life of farming and involvement in the New Hampshire militia's command structure. By the time of the battle of Bunker Hill, Stark was one of the best known military leaders in the colonies and he was most likely the single most successful field commander during the battle as his men annihilated hundreds of British troops at almost no loss to their own forces.

After the end of the Boston campaign, Washington appointed Stark to command an elite corps of sharpshooters which played a major role in the American victories at Trenton and Princeton. However, in early 1777 Stark was superseded on the Continental army promotion list and he resigned his commission to accept command of all New Hampshire militia forces. When Stark was requested to utilize state regiments to counter Burgoyne's invasion from Canada, he agreed only on the condition that he would accept no orders from the Continental Congress. On August 18, 1777, Stark's brigade smashed a large force of Germans and Loyalists at the battle of Bennington and inflicted over 1,000 casualties at a cost of only 30 men lost.

The New Hampshire general rejoined the Continental service late in the war when he was promoted to major general and subsequently emerged as one of the most influential political leaders in his native state. A statue of Stark represents the state of New Hampshire in the United States Capitol.

General Israel Putnam (1718-1790)

Israel Putnam was born in Salem, Massachusetts but moved to Pomfret, Connecticut at age 22 and became a successful farmer and civic leader. In 1756 Putnam was commissioned in the Connecticut provincial forces and was part of the colonial force covering General George Augustus Howe's ill-fated reconnaissance of Fort Ticonderoga. The eldest of the Howe brothers was killed by a French sniper in the action and died in Putnam's arms.

Putnam had an opportunity to switch his commission to the regulars, but instead returned to Pomfret where he combined farming activities with the training of local militia units. By the outbreak of the American Revolution, Putnam was a 57-year-old militia general with an imposing physical presence. One correspondent noted that the general "is a huge man with a bear's body, a bull's voice and an impressive demeanor." He entered the War of Independence with an almost legendary reputation, including narrowly avoiding being burned at the stake by Indians, a shipwreck in a British attempt to capture Havana, a major role in the lifting of Chief Pontiac's siege of Fort Detroit and several harrowing escapes from French captivity.

Putnam was one of the most vocal advocates of American fortification of Charlestown Peninsula and along with William Prescott and John Stark became one of the major figures in the battle. After the Boston campaign, Putnam was placed in command of a division of Continentals and was largely responsible for the rout of the colonial forces in the battle of Long Island. Putnam directed the erection of a formidable series of redoubts which would have produced a decimation of the British similar to Bunker Hill in the event of a frontal assault. However, Howe engineered a huge flanking operation which nearly annihilated the American defenders. Putnam saved a significant part of the Continental army from capture when he executed a daring withdrawal around Howe's lines on Manhattan and linked his forces with Washington's immediate command.

The Connecticut general's roller-coaster career continued for the next year as, along with Nathanael Greene, he correctly advised Washington of the indefensability of Fort Washington, yet several months later failed to hold the Hudson River forts against Sir Henry Clinton's demonstration in favor of Burgoyne's army. Only the subsequent surrender of the British army at Saratoga saved Putnam from an embarrassing disaster. A few months after Saratoga "Old Put" suffered a severe stroke which effectively ended his military career and forced the general into a sedentary lifestyle for the remainder of his life.

CHAPTER VIII

"Dear Bought Victory"
The Tide Turns at Bunker Hill

Sir William Howe had been shocked at the disastrous outcome of the first assault on the rebel positions on Charlestown Peninsula, but he was also convinced that a relatively modest alteration of his operational plan would still carry the field for the Regulars. The general decided to abandon his attempt to catch the enemy in a pincers by pushing his light infantry up Mystic beach; it was now apparent that Stark's stone barricades would be too expensive to capture. Instead, the survivors of the light infantry companies would be used as a reinforcement for the equally decimated grenadier units and the newly merged flank companies would be the shock troops for a new assault on the rail fences. Meanwhile, Howe ordered General Pigot to upgrade his original demonstration attack into a full-fledged assault on the redoubt using every company he could muster.

Howe's newly-refused wing began its second advance, the men still staggering under the weight of full packs and equipment, and now impeded by the bodies of their fallen comrades who littered the approach route. The colonial defenders preparing to meet this second shockwave were now without some of their most notable leaders. While few provincials had been hit by a redcoat firing pattern that was generally far too high to be effective, some bullets had found their mark. Two regimental commanders, colonels Nixon and Brewer, had been wounded badly enough to be forced to leave the field. Nixon's adjutant, Lt. Colonel William Buckminster, was disabled for life with a severe shoulder wound. Captain Isaac Baldwin, one of the most popular New Hampshire company commanders, was hit in the chest, fired three more rounds at the redcoats, and collapsed mortally wounded. But few, if any, American enlisted men were even scratched by the deplorable British marksmanship and the provincial defenders prepared for the new assault with a rising surge of confidence in their ability to defeat the redcoats.

The second British advance proceeded to within 30 yards of the rail fence without a single colonial defender challenging their progress as the only sound that broke the silence of the still afternoon was the music of the Regulars' drummers and fifers. Suddenly, as the redcoats prepared for another bayonet charge, company commanders all along the rebel line shouted "Fire!" in unison and the already decimated British flank companies almost evaporated. The perfectly timed volley mowed down dozens of redcoats in seconds and then, as the elite troops staggered forward, a new scourge appeared. Captain Samuel Everett and a scratch force of volunteer gunners manhandled the two surviving American cannon into position and tore gaping holes in the British ranks. The guns were so well camouflaged that enemy batteries could not put them out of action. As soldiers dropped all around him, Howe ordered the grenadiers to swing to their left in an attempt to flank the rail fence. As the redcoats attempted to swing around a large swampy bog, the colonial troops who had been deployed in the recently constructed fleches suddenly popped up from concealment and poured a withering fusillade on the unsuspecting Regulars. All hope of a successful flanking movement died with dozens of His Majesty's troops.

The elite flank companies of the British army were now essentially finished as fighting formations; at least 450 of 750 light infantry and grenadiers were now dead or severely wounded and many of the survivors had suffered lesser injuries. Now the battalion companies of the 5th and 52nd regiments of foot shoved past their decimated comrades and formed a new assault line. Howe pointed his sword at the American lines and shouted, "Once more men, once more. Show them what English soldiers can do." The Americans responded to this new threat with some of the heaviest firepower of the battle. One British officer noted "as we approached, an incessant stream of fire poured from the rebel lines; it seemed a continual sheet of fire for nearly thirty minutes." This officer was fortunate to be still standing as colonial officers began employing their marksmen in a continuous volley fire in which rear ranks of defenders loaded empty muskets and passed them forward so that the best sharpshooters were able to fire nearly 10 shots a minute, a stupendous rate of fire for 18th-century warfare. Howe was stunned at the volume of fire the "country people" were throwing at his rapidly dwindling army and within a few minutes the general was alone for the second time that day, as every one of the new staff members who had replaced the earlier group was now dead or severely wounded. Although Sir William was still miraculously unhurt, he was shocked by the sight of elite soldiers sprawled by the hundreds along the meadows approaching the enemy rail fences and he admitted later "this was a moment I had never felt before." Most of Howe's men were either dead or retreating back through the high grass and the redcoat general reluctantly turned on his heels and did the unthinkable for a British commander, he left the battlefield with his back to the enemy. When Sir William finally plodded back to Moulton's Point more awful news awaited him; General Pigot's attack had been repulsed in an equally bloody disaster.

General Pigot's second attack was carried out with much the same operational plan as the first attempt with the exception that the Royal Marines and six companies of light infantry and grenadiers were employed to stiffen the assault against the Charlestown side of the American redoubt. However, a wall of colonial fire sent these elite troopers reeling in confusion and allowed Colonel Prescott to resume his skillful shifting of reserves from one threatened front to another. The American commander conceded that the British assault was pressed more energetically than the first attempt. "The enemy advanced and fired very hotly on the fort, and meeting with a warm reception, there was a very smart firing on both sides. After a considerable time, finding our ammunition was almost spent, I commanded a cessation till the enemy advanced again within 30 yards when we gave them such a hot fire that they were obliged to retire nearly one hundred and fifty yards before they could rally."

One of the few redcoats who seemed reluctant to withdraw from this bloody field was General Pigot's adjutant, Major John Small. Major Small was a close friend of Israel Putnam, who had just ridden over from the rail fence to confer with Prescott. The Connecticut general arrived just in time to see his old friend standing almost alone on the field, too proud to either run away or duck from colonial fire. Just as several

Drawing by the noted American military artist H. A. Ogden, perhaps inspired by the encounter between Israel Putnam and Major John Small.

Massachusetts men drew a bead on the solitary redcoat officer, Putnam recognized his friend and knocked up the American guns with his sword shouting, "For God's sake spare that man, I love him as a brother." Small gratefully bowed his thanks at this act of chivalry and withdrew down the slope to the grudging admiration of the colonial defenders.

If General Howe had decided to call off the operation at this moment in time, the battle of Bunker Hill would have rivaled the battle of New Orleans, fought four decades later, as the most one-sided confrontation between British and American armies. The British had lost somewhere between 800 and 900 men in their first two assaults with almost 70 percent of the grenadiers and light infantry either dead or injured to some extent. On the other hand, American casualties during the first two assaults were negligible, probably not much more than a dozen men, roughly the same total suffered by Andrew Jackson's main body at New Orleans. While Howe was stunned by the extent of his losses during such a short period of time, he was still confident that he had far better men than his opponents, and could turn an initial setback into a major British victory before the afternoon was over. Thus when Sir William's surviving subordinates clamored for him to retreat back to Boston, he politely but firmly refused, and instead sent a messenger back to Gage requesting additional reinforcements.

General Howe had directed his messenger to report to Sir Henry Clinton, who was Gage's second in command and had been given authority by the royal governor to determine when reinforcements should be sent to Charlestown. Clinton and General Burgoyne had watched the unfolding drama from the vantage point of Copp's Hill in Boston and the sight of British Regulars fleeing from "country people" filled both men with horror and anger. Clinton, the more emotional of the two generals, was livid with rage when Howe's messenger reported to him with the request for reinforcements, and the former New Yorker flung down his telescope and decided to lead the reinforcing column personally. As the 2nd Battalion of Royal Marines and the 63rd Regiment of Foot boarded the naval barges,

Clinton jumped into the lead boat and ordered them to make all possible speed towards Charlestown Peninsula. Most of the barges made for the main British landing beach at Moulton's Point, but Clinton ordered the midshipman commanding his barge to land near the town of Charlestown. The burning town still contained a few rebel snipers and just as Sir Henry's boat touched shore a soldier next to him keeled over with a bullet wound in his neck. As the general clambered out of the barge another man went down with a mortal chest wound. Clinton ignored the danger of enemy marksmen and surveyed a scene of confusion and helplessness on the beach. Most of the men who had been wounded in Pigot's attack on the redoubt had collected around this beach which was straight down the hill from the British assault route. Some of the men were paralyzed or dying, but others had suffered less crippling head and arm wounds and were sitting in small groups waiting for evacuation to Boston. Clinton immediately exhorted the more mobile casualties to pick up their muskets and join him in another attack. The general noted later, "to their honor, there were many who answered the call," and within a few minutes a dirt-smeared, blood-splattered column of Regulars was ready to follow Sir Henry up the hill toward the redoubt.

While the British assault force was being reorganized and augmented the American defenders were receiving a trickle of reinforcements in their positions. A few individuals had left the security of either Charlestown Common or Bunker Hill to make their way to the front lines and the sight of these brave volunteers cheered at least one original defender to insist, "we are ready for the redcoats again!" Few of the reinforcements carried significant additional powder or balls and the rebels were now dangerously low on ammunition. Most of the colonials had used up their personal supply in the first two assaults, and were now opening unused artillery ammunition to squeeze out a few more rounds. Prescott directed much of this foraging and insisted "not a kernel of powder is to be wasted as we must make certain that every shot should toll." The American commander had just watched Israel Putnam ride back to Bunker Hill to expedite the funneling of men and sup-

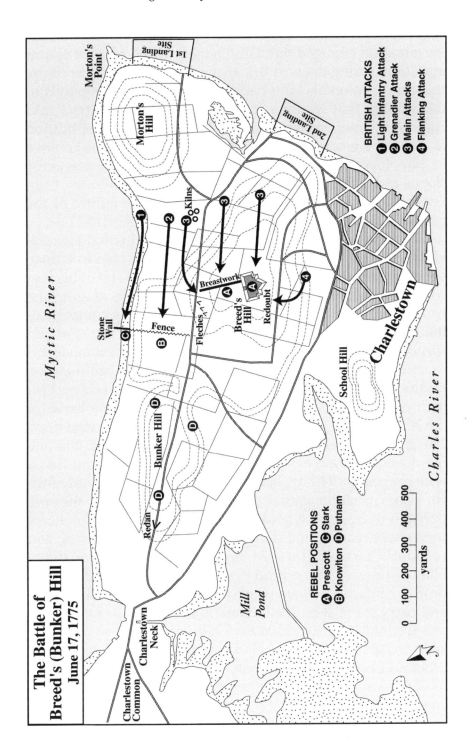

The Battle of
Breed's (Bunker) Hill
June 17, 1775

Morton's
Point

1st Landing
Site

Morton's
Hill

2nd Landing
Site

BRITISH ATTACKS
❶ Light Infantry Attack
❷ Grenadier Attack
❸ Main Attacks
❹ Flanking Attack

Kilns

Breastwork

Fleches

Breed's
Hill

Redoubt

Mystic River

Stone
Wall

Fence

Charlestown

School Hill

Charles River

Bunker Hill

Redan

REBEL POSITIONS
Ⓐ Prescott Ⓒ Stark Ⓓ Putnam

Mill
Pond

Charlestown
Neck

Charlestown
Common

0   100   200   300   400   500
                                yards

N

plies through Charlestown Neck to Breed's Hill but unless the situation changed quickly, his men would run out of ammunition during the next British assault. Prescott ordered the handful of colonials who had bayonets to man the points in the redoubt that were most vulnerable to enemy attack and cheered the few provincials who slipped into the fortification to assist the garrison. However, while thousands of Yankees had deployed from the fields of Charlestown Common to the slopes of Bunker Hill, a relative handful of men in the front line position would determine the success or failure of the climactic part of the battle.

On the south end of Charlestown Peninsula, General Howe was cobbling together a revised attack plan in a final, desperate attempt to carry the rebel works. Several of his best companies were almost eliminated as fighting units in the wake of the first two assaults. The light infantry company of the 35th Regiment of Foot had lost every officer, sergeant and corporal and was now led by a senior private who commanded exactly four men. On the bright side, the proper ammunition for the 6-pounders had now arrived from Boston and Sir William personally placed a number of guns along the banks of the Mystic River within musket range of the American lines. The general expected these pieces to provide vital enfilading fire during the next assault and could now rake the rail fences with grapeshot. The artillery batteries would be the only British forces in action against the fences as Howe made the bold decision to otherwise ignore the rebel left flank and concentrate every man he could deploy against the breastwork and redoubt. This assault would be supported by additional mobile field pieces that would keep the colonials heads' down until the infantry advanced close enough to storm the works and carry them with the bayonet. In order to provide more speed in this vital advance, Sir William ordered all of the assault troops to remove their knapsacks, haversacks and all other non-essential equipment. When a large number of men took this order even more literally and flung aside their red coats, Howe made no objection.

The survivors of the earlier assaults were in no condition

for cheers or huzzas, but they were willing to follow their blood-spattered general on a final march up Breed's Hill. Their commander was now so obsessed with the need for speed and mobility that he decided to initiate the attack without waiting for the disembarking reinforcements to join the assault force. Howe was convinced that the rebels were in the process of pouring reinforcements across Charlestown Neck and, if he waited much longer to capture the redoubt, the American position would become invulnerable. Thus victory or defeat would hinge on what men Sir William had on the field, by this point not much over 1,000 uninjured troops. These surviving Regulars formed ranks and, according to one of Prescott's men "they advanced in open order, the men twelve feet apart in front but very close after one another in extraordinary deep or long files."

Howe's concern for the possibility of being overwhelmed by the colonials milling around Bunker Hill and Charlestown Neck was a reasonable emotion, but Sir William did not realize that the main target of the attack, the redoubt on Breed's Hill, was far more vulnerable than he could imagine. Prescott commanded barely 150 men, who were not receiving significant reinforcements and were now almost out of ammunition. The Massachusetts colonel put up a brave front walking among his men and insisting "if we check them once more they will never come back, the best soldiers in the world cannot take the losses we have given them." However, the commander also knew that if the redcoats ever got inside the fort, his men would be almost helpless against British bayonets and most of the garrison would either surrender or die.

One final time the defenders rested their muskets on the ramparts and pulled their last few rounds from pockets or pouches. The British Regulars, now as much in shirt sleeves as red coats, closed on the redoubt behind a tremendous screen of artillery fire. For a few minutes, the colonials still held out hope of an enormous victory as their last volley cut down dozens of Regulars. As one defender commented, "as fast as the front man was shot down, the next stepped forward into his place, but our men dropped them so fast, they were a long time coming up. It is surprising how they would step over their dead bodies as though they had been logs of wood." The Regulars suffered heavy casualties, but a few minutes later the American fire began to slacken. A number of British officers heard the defenders begin to shout that their powder was all gone, and these commanders now encouraged their men by insisting that their bayonets must soon prevail over the rebels. One officer noted "the men now advanced with infinite spirit to attack the work as their leaders shouted 'push on, push on'."

The Regulars were now in the process of scaling the redoubt walls and, according to 18th-century European custom, the almost helpless defenders could now be expected to capitulate rather than endure the slaughter that could be inflicted by an overwhelming number of attackers. However, the colonials were as emotionally charged as their adversaries and they met the incoming redcoats with clubbed muskets, knives and even fists. A British officer involved in the melee grudgingly expressed his admiration for his opponents as he insisted "there are few instances of Regular troops defending a redoubt till the enemy were up to the very ditches . . . yet I saw several rebels pop their heads and fire even after some of our men were upon the beam." Moments later his men were slashing their way through the defenders "harboring no other feelings but that of revenge."

The British assault force was now dropping into the fort from three directions. General Pigot mounted to one corner of a wall and dropped down to the ground followed by his cheering men. On the opposite wall, the survivors of the 63rd Regiment's company of grenadiers launched a screaming bayonet attack while their senior surviving leader, a junior sergeant, yelled, "we must conquer or die," and began impaling defenders one after another in an action that earned him a rare field commission from Howe. At this point, about 150 defenders were confronting over 1,000 bayonet-wielding Regulars with little more than sheer bravery. A few Americans seized the Regulars' muskets as they clambered over the walls and killed their adversaries with their own bayonets, but there were

British troops overrun the American redoubt on Breed's Hill. The "Liberty or Death" duster on the central figure is well-attested from contemporary sources. The British troops at left with white facings may be Royal Marines.

more redcoats climbing behind them. Marine commander Major John Pitcairn organized his men for a charge from the ramparts, but just as he jumped from a wall the black servant of a Connecticut officer, Salem Prince, fired one of the last American cartridges and mortally wounded the British officer. The last few colonial shots "sputtered out like an old candle" and a moment later "with a huge roar" the main redcoat assault surged forward through the confines of the fort. Marines, grenadiers, light infantrymen and battalion company troops slashed and impaled rebels as the colonists hurled rocks, swung muskets and brandished hatchets or knives in response and, according to one British officer, "fought more like devils than men," but the one-sided engagement was rapidly turning against the defenders. The British assault on Breed's Hill was only coming from three sides, while the rear wall, with its now-vital exit, was not immediately overrun. Thus dozens of colonials could surge out of the redoubt before the redcoats closed the trap. Once the officers commanding the Americans

The climax of the battle. This 19th-century engraving was inspired by Trumbull's painting and is of average accuracy, although it shows to good effect the shoulder "wings" worn by British grenadiers.

Patriot leader Joseph Warren shortly before his fateful stand on Breed's Hill.

deployed along the rail fences realized that any thrust against them was merely a feint, they ordered their best marksmen to shift their fire to cover the now-obvious retreat of their comrades in the redoubt.

Colonel Prescott was soon one of the only uninjured Americans in the improvised fort and he was quickly surrounded by Regulars who thrust at him with their bayonets while he skillfully parried the blows with his sword. The colonel's duster and waistcoat were riddled with holes but he refused to run and instead backed out of the exit still slashing away at his adversaries. On the other hand, Dr. Warren, the highest-ranking provincial officer on the field, was much less fortunate. The socially prominent doctor was one of the most highly-visible men in the colonial army as he was outfitted in an expensive pale blue coat and matching waistcoat. This young physician-turned-politician-turned-soldier managed to retreat out of the redoubt exit at about the same time as Prescott, but other redcoats were now rapidly taking possession of the rear wall and several of them opened fire with a volley that killed Warren and several other retreating Yankees.

A British officer noted that the influential patriot died in his best clothes as "everybody remembers his fine silk fringed waistcoat."

Once the Regulars gained control of the walls, American casualties rose dramatically. Colonel Gridley was wounded as he retreated toward Bunker Hill, while at least one regimental commander was killed leading a relief force down that same hill. Meanwhile, despite General Putnam's efforts to transform Bunker Hill into a new front line, a continuous stream of shells from the Royal Navy vessels created chaos among the defenders who were huddling behind rocks or trees and unwilling to deploy long enough to challenge the British advance from Breed's Hill.

The British assault force had now achieved its primary objective, capture of the American redoubt, but an immediate advance up Bunker Hill was seriously challenged by Stark's New Hampshire men and Knowlton's Connecticut contingent. These men continued to pour accurate volleys into the enemy flank. Even when it was clear that the redoubt was lost, Stark ordered the men to save the two remaining cannon and conducted a fighting withdrawal. The redcoats were equally determined to capture the rebel field pieces as a tangible symbol of their bloody victory and the result was a wild melee. The colonials responsible for rescuing the artillery pieces were men from Charlestown who had just watched their homes burned to the ground, and these infuriated Yankees picked off redcoats until they were almost overwhelmed by perhaps 10 times their number. Although one cannon was finally abandoned, the other piece was dragged out of harm's way in a vicious rearguard action.

Stark's men were finally giving ground, but so grudgingly that even the British officers were highly impressed. General Burgoyne, still watching the battle from Copp's Hill, focused his telescope on the rebel left flank and admitted, "the retreat was no flight, it was even covered with bravery and military skill." The combination of Stark's timely covering fire for the defenders of the redoubt and his skillful withdrawal dramatically reduced British opportunities to take prisoners and at the end of the battle only 30 Americans, most of them severely wounded, were in enemy hands.

The focal point of the action now shifted from Breed's Hill to the ridge for which the battle would ultimately be named— Bunker Hill. As the defenders of the American front line re- treated up the slopes of Bunker Hill, colonial reinforcements deployed along the bottom of the hill to slow down the British tide. Colonel Thomas Gardner deployed his regiment behind trees and fences at the foot of the hill and his men's excellent marksmanship bought time for their comrades to sprint up a nearby road to the temporary safety of the crest. However, Gardner went down with a fatal wound and the path to the top was soon open to the redcoats. Individuals and small groups of colonials fought a vicious battle against the Regu- lars for possession of the crest of Bunker Hill, but Putnam was never able to organize the coherent deployment of men that might have stopped the advancing British companies in their tracks. American resistance began to crumble and a relentless series of bayonet attacks finally pushed the last rebel defend- ers down the rear slope of Bunker Hill in open retreat toward Charlestown Neck and the safety of the mainland.

Howe was now a victorious general with a serious di- lemma; should he halt the British advance and congratulate his men on their triumph, or roll the dice another time and attempt to push the Americans back to Cambridge before nightfall? General Clinton, who had been heavily involved in the final assault, urged Howe to push past Charlestown Neck to the mainland, as he was convinced that the whole rebel army would disintegrate after one more taste of British steel. Sir William believed that the colonials would be just as vulner- able the next morning. The British general was also stunned by the extent of casualties among his men and fervently hoped that the retreating provincial army would evaporate without the need for another gory redcoat assault. Thus at five o'clock on this Saturday afternoon, a British flag was posted on Bun- ker Hill and Royal Artillery batteries were trundled up the slopes to fire shots across the Neck to the mainland. As the exhausted colonial troops threw up additional earthworks on

Winter Hill and Prospect Hill, the British Regulars made no attempt to pursue them.

Colonel Prescott, who was far bolder than General Howe and indignant at the lack of support when victory seemed nearly in the Americans' grasp, rode to Cambridge and angrily confronted Artemus Ward. While Ward profusely thanked his subordinate for the fine showing of the front line troops, he refused to give Prescott the 1,500 men the colonel insisted would be sufficient to retake the peninsula in a night assault on the redcoats. The American commanding general was still concerned that the British would attack Cambridge sometime that night or early Sunday morning and Prescott left provincial headquarters, according to one witness "feeling as he had not yet done enough to satisfy his country." Across the Charles River in Boston, the equally energetic and daring British subordinate, Sir Henry Clinton, fumed at his commander's refusal to order a night attack and wrote an impassioned letter to a friend in England emphasizing the futility of that Saturday's operations by insisting "this was truly a dear bought victory, another such victory would have ruined us."

Colonel William Prescott (1726-1795)

William Prescott was the son of the Honorable Benjamin Prescott, a large landholder and justice of the peace in Groton, Massachusetts. At age 19 Prescott enlisted in the provincial army to participate in King George's War, was present at the capture of Louisburg, and was a lieutenant in a company of colonial infantry in the attack on Cape Breton. His exploits during the colonial wars gained the attention of British leaders and he was subsequently offered a commission in the regular army, an invitation he turned down to undertake a career in farming. When Britain's Port Bill closed Boston Harbor to most shipping, the gentleman farmer organized overland delivery of food supplies to the city while simultaneously taking command of a regiment of provincial militia. During the British retreat from the raid on Concord, Prescott's command nearly cut off General Percy's retreat and the colonel's actions were prominent enough to gain him a seat on the provincial army's Council of War by late April of 1775.

Prescott emerged from the battle of Bunker Hill as a hero throughout the colonies and was given important command assignments by General Washington during the remainder of the siege. During the subsequent campaign in New York, Prescott organized a number of skillful retreats under difficult conditions and was publicly commended by Washington on several occasions. He was among the key officers, along with Benedict Arnold and Daniel Morgan, sent by Washington to Horatio Gates' Northern Army in the wake of Burgoyne's invasion from Canada, and Prescott played an active role on Gates' staff in the period leading to the British surrender at Saratoga. At this point the 51-year-old patriot leader returned to a command in the Massachusetts state forces, a position he held through the end of the war and through the military activities surrounding Shay's Rebellion. By the time of his death in 1795, Prescott was a virtual legend throughout the new nation and was lauded as a major hero of the Revolution. Daniel Webster noted, ". . . if it were proper to give a battle [Bunker Hill] any name, from any distinguished agents in it, it should be called Prescott's battle."

Prescott's only son, William, Jr., became a state senator and prominent judge, while his grandson, William Hickling Prescott, a well-known writer, married the granddaughter of Captain Linzee who commanded the British sloop of war *Falcon*, which had fired at the colonel while he stood on Breed's Hill redoubt. The newly married couple celebrated their union by placing the crossed swords of Prescott and Linzee on the library wall of their home near Boston in the 1840's.

Dr. Joseph Warren (1740-1775)

Joseph Warren, who died in the closing moments of the British assault on Breed's Hill, was the highest ranking officer killed on either side during the Boston campaign. Warren had just been appointed by the Massachusetts Provincial Congress as major general and commanding officer of all provincial forces, but he refused to exercise that rank during the battle of Bunker Hill.

Warren was born on May 29, 1740, in Roxbury, Massachusetts, the son of 41-year-old Joseph Warren, Senior and 29-year-old Mary Stevens. Warren's father was a prosperous farmer who died when the future patriot leader was 14 years old, but his widowed mother was able to scrape together enough money to send her son to Harvard. Warren then apprenticed himself to Dr. James Lloyd, a prominent Boston physician, and during the smallpox epidemic of 1763 the two men emerged as heroes of the community for their efforts in holding down the death rate. The young doctor soon became grand master of Boston's Masonic community and personal physician to most of the town's leading families. In 1764 he married 18-year-old Elizabeth Hooton, daughter of a wealthy merchant, and the couple had four children before the death of the wife in 1772, an event which happened the same week as the death of Paul Revere's first wife.

By the spring of 1775, Warren had emerged as one of the most influential spokesmen for the patriot cause, and his keynote address at the fifth anniversary commemoration of the Boston Massacre almost provoked hostilities between British officers and local townspeople present at the event.

During the British retreat from Concord, Warren was heavily involved in the fighting and just missed a fatal wound on several occasions. After the battle, Warren was appointed president of the Massachusetts Provincial Congress and subsequently named a major general of the colony's militia forces.

At the battle of Bunker Hill, Warren deferred to Colonel Prescott's authority at the battle site and was killed as one of the last men retiring from the redoubt. Warren was buried by Captain Walter Lurie, who had been senior British officer at North Bridge, Concord, two months earlier. Lurie noted, "I stuffed the scoundrel with another rebel into one hole and there he and his seditious principles may remain." After the British evacuation of Boston, Paul Revere exhumed Warren's corpse and identified the body through the artificial teeth that he had wired into the doctor's jaw just before Bunker Hill. Revere named his next son Joseph Warren Revere.

Naming a Battle—The Controversy of "Bunker Hill" vs. "Breed's Hill"

One of the most famous battles in American history also produced one of the longest running disputes over the authentic name of the site of the engagement. While the term Bunker Hill was listed in Charlestown deeds and town records for decades before 1775, the term Breed's Hill was not named in any official documents but appears to have been one of several designations for the hill and meadows in the middle of Charlestown Peninsula. Locals also called the central part of the peninsula Russel's Pasture, Green's Pasture and Breed's Pasture, while British maps designated the site as Green's Hill.

When the Massachusetts Committee of Safety was debating the occupation and fortification of Charlestown Peninsula, General Artemus Ward listed the advantages and liabilities of fortifying Charlestown Hill which technically could have been any of the three elevations on the peninsula. Ward's account of the battle was called "the Battle of Charlestown" while John Stark's account to the New Hampshire legislature noted that the patriots entrenched on Charlestown Hill. The Massachusetts Provincial Congress' report to the Continental Congress noted that the patriots had built a redoubt "on a small hill south of Bunker Hill." Patriot chaplain Rev. John Martin wrote an account of the battle for President Ezra Stiles of Yale College in which he called the entire engagement "the battle of Bunker's Hill," while British newspapers featured stories about "the battle of Bunker Hill, near Charlestown, in New England."

The first significant designation of the engagement as the battle of Breed's Hill did not occur until 1816 when former general James Wilkinson, who was not present at the battle, wrote a description of "the battle of Breed's Hill" as part of a larger volume on the War of Independence. The matter was further confused by the fact that Stark and Knowlton's forces behind the rail fences were actually occupying ground that was considered the base of Bunker Hill and the British assault against their position was one of the major elements of the battle. The importance of this part of the engagement, combined with the fact that British followed up their capture of Prescott's redoubt with an assault up Bunker Hill itself, indicates that the naming of the contest as the "battle of Bunker Hill" is not really as erroneous as some purists have indicated.

CHAPTER IX

Aftermath of Bunker Hill
Howe and Washington
Assume Command

Hours after the British flag was planted on Bunker Hill, General Thomas Gage penned a glowing account of the battle to his superiors in London. However, this technical British victory so decimated the army in Boston that it created a sense of shock and horror throughout the British government and society. The capture of Charlestown Peninsula had cost the Regular army almost half of the assault force as the 2,300 men who actually fought on that torrid Saturday afternoon suffered 1,054 casualties including 226 men killed, compared to a colonial total of 140 killed and 271 wounded. The British losses included a fearsomely high toll of officers, as 100 men holding the king's commission were either dead or permanently out of action due to the bloody assaults; thus about 25 percent of the British officers corps in North America was effectively eliminated in a single afternoon. Gage's official report blithely ignored the implications of these numbers as the royal governor insisted, "the superiority of the King's troops, who under every disadvantage, attacked and defeated over three times their number, strongly posted in breastworks, was clearly demonstrated." William Eden, an assistant to a cabinet minister, summarized the hopes and fears that Gage's report had stirred among Britons. "We certainly are victorious in the engagement of the 17th, but if we have eight more such victories, there will be nobody left to bring news of them. It is certainly not that brilliant and decisive success which we were taught to look for, but yet it is a success so far as it goes and not unlikely in the event to make the rebels sick of their undertaking."

While Eden personified the mixed feelings of many British officials over the "victory" at Bunker Hill, the one person who mattered the most, King George III, reveled in the accomplishments of Sir William Howe, even if showing far less enthusiasm for his superior, General Gage. The king portrayed Bunker Hill as an example of what properly trained British Regulars could do to amateur militia and convinced himself that only substantial reinforcement of military power in America could bring the "deluded provincials" to their senses. "I am clear as to one point," the king affirmed, "that we must persist and not be dismayed by any difficulties that may arise on either side of the Atlantic. I know I am doing my duty and therefore can never wish to retreat." The monarch essentially gave Lord North and his cabinet a blank check to use whatever force was necessary to crush the rebels and ordered his first minister and his associates to develop a plan to bring the American provinces back under royal authority in the shortest time possible.

Within a week after Gage's dispatches had arrived in England, the British cabinet had hammered out a detailed strategy for effectively deploying the bulk of the British army in the suppression of the growing colonial rebellion. While a number of 20th-century Americans have assumed that the ultimate defeat of Britain implies a half-hearted imperial response to the rebels, the real situation was far different. Lord North and his military advisors almost immediately stripped Ireland of much of its garrison and sent five of the best regiments in that country to reinforce Gage in Boston. By July 31 the War Office was already arranging the embarkation of these troops while the cabinet was busy authorizing a massive expansion of the British military establishment in America. Each regiment already stationed in the colonies would receive enough individual recruits to deploy 811 men in the field, more than double their normal strength, as all new enlistees in England, Scotland and Ireland would be posted for duty in America. Over and above this augmentation, an additional 20,000 men would be embarked for the colonies by the spring of 1776, as garrisons all over the empire were stripped to provide fighting men. Lord North, who is often portrayed as the epitome of the cautious bureaucrat, actually outran his ministers in enthusiasm for decisive action. The first minister proposed the immediate dispatch of nine additional regiments from the home garrison of England to Massachusetts before the Atlantic weather deteriorated, in order to enable the Regulars to launch a major fall campaign designed to push the rebels away from Boston and into the interior of the province where they could be destroyed at leisure. Even the normally hard-line Secretary at War, Lord Barrington, shuddered at this proposal, as it would leave only 2,000 first line infantry to defend all of England against either a local insurrection or the ever-present danger of French invasion.

The cabinet ministers were able to convince the prime minister to postpone his audacious and risky plan to strip the realm of troops in order to crush the rebels in an early campaign, but they agreed with North that the largest expeditionary force to embark from Britain's shores should be set in motion as early as was militarily feasible. Three methods of substantially augmenting the available pool of manpower were approved. First, militia units in England would be deployed to take over the garrison duties of Regular regiments in the home islands, thus freeing additional Regulars for duty in America. Second, recruiting practices in the United Kingdom would be expanded to allow reduced levels of physical standards, increased use of bounties, pardoning of convicted criminals and acceptance of larger quotas of Irish Catholics, all designed to entice larger numbers of subjects to accept the king's shilling and don the red coat. Finally, substantial numbers of conscripts serving in German principalities such as Hesse and Brunswick would be hired by Britain to augment troops embarking from the British Isles.

These almost draconian measures of military expansion would provide the British commander in America with an impressive army of over 30,000 men by the late spring of 1776, but both George III and his ministers were increasingly convinced that General Gage should not be that leader. After the controversial Bunker Hill engagement, Gage's reputation was in free fall at home and the monarch and his advisors agreed that the royal governor should be called home for "consultations," rewarded for his service with additional honors and titles and replaced with a more aggressive field command. Sir William Howe had impressed the king and his ministers through his aggressive, if costly, drive on Breed's Hill, and the cabinet agreed to assign him the command of the forces deployed around Boston.

Howe's warrant as commanding general did not provide him with authority over Governor Guy Carleton's Quebec garrison, but did give the general "full authority to act according to your own judgment and discretion" in operations in Massachusetts with the single proviso that "the Loyalists in Boston must not be abandoned to the rage and insults of the rebels" and that "effectual care be taken for the protection of Halifax, which, being the great repository of all our naval stores, is an object of the first importance." While the new commander was technically free to choose his own strategy to defeat the rebels, the cabinet ministers suggested three possible methods to prosecute the war. The first possible strategy was to confine operations to New England for the foreseeable future, using Boston as a base for offensives into the Massachusetts countryside. A second option was to abandon Boston or hold the city with only a small garrison and move the bulk of the army to New York in an attempt to split the northern and southern axis of colonial resistance. Finally, Howe could initiate an offensive somewhere other than Massachusetts or New York if he felt he could "gain a superior advantage and safety and convenience for the British army." Sir William immediately began to consider the various alternative strategies, probably with one eye focused on military feasibility and the other eye focused on how the plan would enhance his own reputation in England. However, while the new British commander poured over his maps and consulted his senior officers, events in Cambridge and Philadelphia would ultimately produce a new adversary for Sir William and his eventual successors.

The day before Colonel Prescott's men began their fortification of Charlestown Peninsula, the Continental Congress chose a new commander in chief for the rebel army deployed around Boston. The president of Congress, John Hancock, hoped and expected to be offered the command of an army that was still almost exclusively composed of New Englanders. The Boston merchant believed that a combination of his service as colonel of that city's most elite militia unit, his status as one of the most notable leaders of the patriot movement and the influence garnered by his enormous wealth suited him ideally for the newly authorized position of general in chief of the Grand American Army. However, Hancock's fellow Massachusetts delegate John Adams was equally determined that the only chance for a New England uprising to expand into a continent-wide revolution was the appointment of a commanding general from a region outside of New England who might

The support of New Englander John Adams was crucial in getting Virginian George Washington the command of the Continental forces.

stimulate other colonies into closer alliance with their northern counterparts. Adams had picked out his candidate early in the Congressional sessions and his choice was, coincidentally, the only delegate wearing a military uniform at every meeting, Colonel George Washington of Virginia.

The nomination of George Washington to the post of "General and Commander in Chief of all the forces raised and to be raised in defense of liberty" proved to be a happy convergence of interests for key northern and southern members of the Continental Congress. On the one hand, a number of prominent New Englanders admitted that there was not a better means of obtaining vital southern support for the army besieging Boston than by choosing a man from that region to be the supreme commander. Even northern delegates noted Washington's impressive appearance and his excellent record serving in the military committees of Congress. Compared to men with relatively similar military rank and experience, no other single individual gave evidence of the same well-rounded personality, steadfast character and political sagacity displayed by the owner of Mount Vernon plantation. While northerners viewed the Virginian's appointment as a device to attract more broad-based support for the army deployed in Massachusetts, men from the South saw Washington as a barrier to New England's ongoing threat to dominate all of North America. Many influential patriots from New York to Georgia were uneasy about the prospect of the New England army defeating and expelling the British and then imposing their own peculiar laws and lifestyle on the rest of the colonies. The appointment of Washington would serve as a deterrent against the possibility of substituting King Stork for King Log.

The selection of Washington was virtually unanimous, but his appointment opened up a complex debate over the list of subordinate generals for the newly emerging American army. The senior major-generalship almost automatically went to Artemus Ward since he was the senior New England general and currently commanded the main field army. The third spot, second-ranking major general, went to the most professionally experienced candidate available, Englishman Charles

George Washington in the uniform of the French and Indian War, his main source of military experience.

Lee, who had commanded a regiment of Regulars in the French and Indian War, had served as a major general in the Polish army and had recently settled in Virginia as a country squire. Before Lee had moved to America, he had enthusiastically supported the grievances of the colonists against the British government and had even insulted the king to his face about his colonial policies. Thus when the former British officer settled in Virginia, he was quickly befriended by influential patriots, including George Washington who had known him during the French and Indian War.

Lee's appointment as third officer in the American army was particularly important since Artemus Ward was in precarious health and had no great desire to continue serving in an army that he no longer commanded. Thus if Washington was killed or captured, the future of the patriot cause would be on the shoulders of a man who had only recently arrived in

America. While Washington and Lee got along well during the Boston campaign and even for most of the ensuing campaign in New York, they were almost polar opposites. Washington was well-dressed, handsome and generally congenial in a social gathering. Lee was possibly the most eccentric general serving in either army during the War of Independence. The Englishman was unwashed, foul-mouthed, boastful, long-winded and egotistical. He admitted that he preferred the company of dogs to people and generally kept five or six canines in his office or bedroom. There is little doubt that he considered himself far superior to Washington in military talent and accepted the major general's commission mainly as a stepping stone to army command in the not-too-distant future. Yet at this point in time, Lee very much had his superior's ear as they traveled together to Boston and for better or worse, his ideas would influence Washington as he directed the next phase of the Boston campaign.

As Washington prepared for his journey from Philadelphia to Cambridge, congress finalized the list of senior commissions in the new army, and they reflected more interest in geographical balance than potential leadership qualities. Fellow member of congress Philip Schuyler was given the third major general's commission in deference to his wealth and influence in New York and the strategic location of the colony. The colorful and well-known Israel Putnam was given the final set of two stars designating major general. Eight brigadier commissions were also issued, and in this category the New Englanders received heavy representation with Seth Pomeroy, Richard Montgomery, David Wooster, William Heath, Joseph Spencer, John Thomas, John Sullivan and Nathanael Greene forming a corps of brigadiers that included seven natives of the four northern colonies. However, both Spencer and Thomas fumed at alleged slights in the order of seniority of the new generals as Spencer insisted that he outranked Israel Putnam in the New England army while Thomas lambasted Congress for giving Pomeroy seniority over himself when he was currently commander of the largest wing of the besieging army. Spencer agreed to accept his commission only after Seth

Pomeroy's retirement opened up the senior brigadier post and Thomas was only prevented from resigning by the emotional pleas of Washington, who also apparently held out the entice-ment of advancement later in the campaign. The final general's commission was specifically requested by the new army com-mander, who asked Congress to appoint transplanted English-man Horatio Gates as his adjutant general with the rank of brigadier. Gates, the illegitimate son of a duke and his house-keeper, held the rank of major in the British army until the early 1770's when, like Lee, he emigrated to Virginia and de-veloped a friendship with Washington. Ironically, Lee and Gates would emerge as two of the new commander's bitterest critics in coming campaigns. Washington's final additions to his official "family" included two more fellow members of the Continental Congress. Joseph Reed was induced to accept the title of the general's military secretary and Thomas Mifflin was appointed aide-de-camp. Thus as the new general pre-pared to leave for Massachusetts, his staff of key advisors and subordinates included three fellow members of Congress and two English born neighbors in Virginia, apparently a friendly and congenial group to accompany the general in his perilous new assignment. However, four of these five men would ulti-mately turn against Washington while among the seemingly alien New Englanders men such as Nathanael Greene and Henry Knox would emerge as his staunchest supporters.

On June 21, 1775, four days after the battle of Bunker Hill, General Washington set out from Philadelphia with a stream of vehicles and mounted escorts that soon created the image of a triumphal procession. By the time he had reached Cam-bridge on July 2, he had been saluted, feted, toasted and complimented dozens of times. Even the Provincial Congress of Massachusetts used decidedly un-New England-like flat-tery to welcome the general. "While we applaud that atten-tion to the public good manifested in your appointment, we equally admire that disinterested virtue and distinguished patriotism, which alone could call you from those enjoyments of domestic life, which a sublime and manly taste, joined with a most affluent fortune, can afford, to hazard your life and to endure the fatigues of war, in defense of the rights of mankind and the good of your country."

The next morning, July 3, 1775, 42 picked drummers and fifers marched in line and accompanied Artemus Ward and Washington to an official inspection of three assembled regiments. One officer wrote home that the ceremony of Ward turning over his command to the new general "was one of a great deal of grandeur" while a subsequent reception for Washington in the former commander's headquarters included "rollicking bachelor's songs, calculated to make the immobile features of the chief relax, glasses clinked, stories were told and the wine circulated." The next morning, in the spirit of the conviviality of the evening before, Washington replied to the welcome of both the Massachusetts legislature and the New England officers. He insisted that his willingness to give up the comfort of private life "only emulates the virtue and public spirit of the whole province of Massachusetts Bay, which, with a firmness and patriotism without example in modern

Washington takes command. Although somewhat idealized, the drawing accurately depicts the total lack of uniformity of American troops at the time.

history, has sacrificed all the comforts of social and political life in support of the rights of mankind and the welfare of our common country. My highest ambition is to the happy instrument of vindicating those rights and to see this devoted province once again restored to peace, liberty and safety."

Washington's public addresses exuded confidence in the certainty of eventual success and the virtues of the New Englanders he commanded. His private correspondence revealed a very different tone. A letter to one friend insisted "our lines are fourteen miles in extent and I am scamperer General. I am seldom less than twelve hours on horseback. The want of engineers has occassioned a fatigue in me scarcely credible. I do not believe there is one capable of constructing an oven." Washington admitted that his new army was well-fed and reasonably healthy given the rudimentary sanitary conditions in the camp, but he also noted that most of the troops "are the most indifferent people I ever saw. . . . exceedingly dirty and nasty people." The Virginian was appalled by the leveling spirit of the northerners as was particularly evident in the relationship between officers and enlisted men. "Officers are nearly of the same kidney of the privates as they eat and sleep in complete equality. If a captain happens to be a barber in civilian life, he shaves his soldiers in camp."

Washington almost immediately ordered his officers to wear colored ribbons on their shirts or coats to denote their rank. While this tactic produced some distancing of officers and enlisted men it had no impact on another equally serious problem—the relation between the senior New England officers and the new arrivals from Philadelphia. While Artemus Ward was civil to his replacement, he never forgave Congress for superseding him with no consultation and played virtually no role in the remainder of the campaign. Lee's pomposity was particularly galling to the New England generals when they observed his easy access to the commanding general, a courtesy that did not seem to extend to them to nearly the same degree. The commanding general indeed might now be a southerner, but beyond a token force of riflemen from Pennsylvania and Maryland, the "Grand American Army" remained very much a New England organization that happened to have a Virginian at its head.

Washington had been told before he left Philadelphia that he was riding north to take command of an army of over 20,000 men, but when the new general perused the rolls of the various regiments, he discovered that only 13,000 troops were actually present and fit for duty. Meanwhile a steady stream of British reinforcements reaching Boston had pushed the garrison to 22 regiments and several battalions of marines, creating an aggregate of over 10,000 men. The shock of the near parity of the rival armies was amplified dramatically when Washington double checked the available ammunition supply. When the Virginian had arrived, he had been informed that 308 barrels of gunpowder were available in a string of provincial storehouses around the periphery of the American lines. However, when the general began requesting extra ammunition for his most forward units, he was startled to find there were only 36 barrels on hand, an amount that would provide only nine rounds per man in the event of a British offensive. Apparently the original figure had been tabulated before the battle of Bunker Hill, an engagement that had all but exhausted the provincial powder supply. Washington was forced to send cryptic messages to Congress pleading for more powder while couching the requests in vague generalities in case the dispatches were intercepted by the British who would then be almost sure to launch an all-out offensive against an army that would be almost unable to defend itself.

The Virginia general met secretly with leaders of the Massachusetts provincial congress to request a combing of every town's powder houses for emergency supplies while orders quietly made their way to ordnance officers to begin constructing hundreds of spears to be issued to the men if a British attack seemed likely. Washington also initiated a program of disinformation towards the British that would be utilized repeatedly during the next six or seven years. In this case, the general leaked word to British headquarters that he was almost embarrassed to find that the Massachusetts legislature had supplied him with 1,800 barrels of powder which was unfortunately causing storage problems for his overworked supply officers. The same leak also explained that Washington had recently imposed a ban on random firing in the camp on the grounds that this activity weakened discipline and elicited the ridicule of the enemy. The British staff accepted this information as genuine, congratulated themselves on their first-rate intelligence service, and ordered their men to remain on the defensive rather than assault an enemy army that allegedly fielded 20,000 men and had almost limitless access to ammunition.

Once the powder crisis was at least temporarily resolved through additional shipments from Philadelphia, Washington started to restructure the American army in anticipation of offensive operations in the near future. The first priority was to reorganize the officer corps, which had a makeup that simply appalled the hierarchically-oriented Virginian. Washington was determined to establish a cadre of officers who would have the authority, status and ability to discipline and train the colonial soldiers to a level where they could meet the redcoats on an equal basis on the battlefield. He noted that his own experiences in Virginia plantation society convinced him that "gentlemen of fortune and respectable families generally make the most useful officers" and insisted that "the person commanded yields but reluctant obedience to those he concludes are undeservedly made his superior." The general also believed that talent for leadership had to be complemented by a proper appearance and so he urged Congress to raise the pay of junior officers "so they may support the character and appearance of officers" and be able to keep their distance from the men they expected to command.

By late summer of 1775, Washington's reorganization of the American army was beginning to become a noticeable event among both the soldiers affected and civilian spectators. The general wrote to fellow Virginian Richard Henry Lee, "I have made a pretty good slam among such kind of officers as the Massachusetts government abound in, since I came to the camp, having broke one colonel and two captains for cowardly behavior in the action at Bunker Hill, two captains for drawing more provisions and pay than they had men in their company, and one for being absent from his post when the enemy appeared. Besides these, I have at this time one colonel, one major, one captain and two subalterns under arrest for trial. In short, I spare none, yet fear it will not all do as these people seem to be too inattentive to everything but their interest."

Regimental chaplain Reverend William Emerson of Concord viewed Washington's activities from the perspective of a native New Englander. "There is a great overturning in the camp as to order and regularity. New lords, new laws. The Generals Washington and Lee are upon the lines every day. Great distinction is made between officers and soldiers. Everyone is made to know his place and keep it or be tied up and receive thirty or forty lashes according to his crime." The army was now beginning to take on the characteristics of a more professional force that Washington insisted was necessary if the colonials had any chance to beat the British Regulars in a conventional battle. However, as cold weather descended on the Massachusetts countryside, the new commander's desire to utilize his upgraded army to chase the redcoats out of Boston began to collide with the reality of limited opportunities to engage the British on anything like favorable terms. Several months of frustrating stalemate would pass before the aggressive Virginian finally had his opportunity for a showdown with the new British adversary, Sir William Howe.

Appointment of George Washington as Commanding General

When George Washington arrived at the opening session of the Second Continental Congress in the spring of 1775, he was the only member wearing a military uniform. Despite his public protestations about his unfitness to command the colonial army, Washington was probably very interested in the appointment but felt it was beneath his dignity to openly campaign for the post. Washington's main competitors for the position were probably transplanted Englishman Charles Lee and Massachusetts political leader John Hancock, who was currently serving as president of the Congress. The Virginian's major liability was his lack of any substantial military victory under his direct command while defeats at Fort Necessity and near Fort Duquesne produced some questions among the delegates. However, Washington's chief rivals carried even more potential liabilities. Charles Lee had only resided in America for a short time and his most notable command position, major general in the Polish army, held little credibility for American congressmen. Hancock had never commanded any troops in battle, and was generally viewed as more of an asset at his president's

desk than as a military leader.

The probable key development in Washington's appointment occurred when Massachusetts delegate John Adams nominated the Virginian for the post in a particularly glowing speech, and then was seconded on the nomination by his cousin Samuel Adams. Ironically, the principal opposition to Washington's appointment came from fellow Virginian Edmund Pendleton, who challenged the delegates to name a single military victory that the nominee had won. Washington had previously sequestered himself in the State House library to avoid influencing the tenor of the debate and when he was ushered back into the main meeting room and offered the post of commander in chief, he insisted, "I do not think myself equal to the command I am honored with," and refused to accept a salary for his services. His official commission from Congress was "General and Commander in Chief of the forces raised and to be raised in defense of American liberty," a position that gave him supreme field command but maintained subordination to Congress outside the battlefield.

Artemus Ward (1727-1800)

Ward was the son of a selectman and justice of the peace in Shrewsbury, Massachusetts who had made a fortune as the master of a slave ship in the West Indies. Artemus entered Harvard College in 1744 with a social ranking that placed him seventh in a class of 29. After graduation, he married a descendant of the powerful Mather and Cotton families and at the outbreak of the French and Indian War was offered a commission as a major in the Third Volunteer Regiment of Massachusetts. Ward spent most of the war supervising the raising, organizing and equipping of the Massachusetts provincial forces but did command a regiment next to Thomas Gage's unit in a failed attack on Fort Ticonderoga.

Soon after the war, Ward was appointed to the Governor's Council, the upper body of the Massachusetts legislature, but his patriot sympathies increasingly antagonized the royal governor. When the colonial legisla-

ture was replaced with a Provincial Congress, Ward was elected to the powerful Committee of Safety and named commander in chief of all Massachusetts forces.

After the appointment of George Washington as senior general in the Continental army, Ward served as second in command of the field army and directed one wing of the army on a day to day basis. After the British evacuation of Boston, Ward remained in Massachusetts as commander of the Eastern Department of the Continental army, a post he held until his election to the Continental Congress in 1780.

Ward was not highly regarded by either Washington or Charles Lee, but was extremely popular in New England and was believed to have held the colonial army together during one of the most crucial periods of the War of Independence. Ward died of a stroke in October of 1800, 10 months after the death of Washington.

CHAPTER X

A Season of Stalemate

When George Washington arrived in Cambridge in July of 1775, he anticipated a brief period of acclimatization to his new command, followed by a major offensive designed to either annihilate the British army in Boston or at least drive the redcoats from the city. However, most of his advisors immediately began to urge caution in dealing with a British army that could be lethal if underestimated. One general insisted to Washington, "the British position is surrounded with ships of war, floating batteries, etc., and the narrow necks of land leading to them are fortified in such a manner as not to be forced without very considerable slaughter, if carried at all." Thus the Virginian marked time, reorganizing his army while hoping that his British adversary would make some critical error that would enable the colonials to confront the Regulars under conditions favorable to the American army.

This army was now arranged in three grand divisions, each consisting of two brigades containing a total of 12 or 13 regiments in which men from the same colony were grouped together as often as possible. Artemus Ward, still miffed at being shunted down to second in command and often in pre-carious health, was given command of the right-wing division of the army, which included a brigade of seven regiments

British sketch of American lines on Boston Neck. Dorchester Heights is visible at left.

of Massachusetts troops under General John Thomas, and a mixed brigade of three Massachusetts regiments and three Connecticut regiments all under the command of General Joseph Spencer. This division was deployed in the vicinity of Roxbury and faced a strong British contingent deployed around Boston Neck. The left wing of the army was entrusted to General Charles Lee, who was assigned command of General John Sullivan's brigade of three New Hampshire regiments and three Massachusetts regiments and General Nathanael Greene's brigade of three Rhode Island and four Massachusetts regiments. Lee made his headquarters at Prospect Hill across Charlestown Neck from Bunker Hill. The center division, under General Israel Putnam, was stationed at Cambridge and included General William Heath's brigade of six Massachusetts regiments and a second brigade of one Connecticut and five Massachusetts regiments which remained temporarily under Putnam's direct command until Washington could appoint a new brigadier. These 38 infantry regiments, with a paper strength of 16,770 men, were augmented by a regiment of artillery including 489 men under Colonel Richard Gridley and a single-independent company of Rhode Island artillery deploying an additional 96 men. Thus just under 17,400 men were on the rolls of the Grand American Army, although the large number of men home on leave, sick, or simply deserted cut about 4,000 from this total on any given day.

The colonial army was deployed in a giant crescent focused primarily on preventing the British army from successfully launching offensive operations from either Boston Neck or Charlestown Neck. Observers on both sides of the lines noted the irony that such a beautiful countryside was now the focal point of an increasingly bloody war. An American writer commented that, "the unrivaled natural scenery could not pass unobserved by a lover of nature" yet, "now the beautiful hills are covered with the pomp and pride of war." A British officer concurred with this viewpoint, noting, "the country is most beautifully tumbled about in hills and valleys, rocks and woods, interspersed with straggling villages, with here and there a spire peeping over the trees, and the country of the most charming green that delighted eye ever gazed on." The beautiful hills that surrounded the key passes of Boston Neck and Charlestown Neck were now dotted with white tents and gleaming brass cannon while in the nearby water "no small

Contemporary view of the British garrison in Boston under siege.

portion of the navy of England rides proudly in the harbor." Occasionally the tedium of the siege was brightened when either British or Americans staged a review of their forces or initiated a sharp skirmish to gain a small advantage somewhere along the lines. However, most of the fall and early winter were spent in patrolling and digging fortifications. Reverend William Emerson noted, "thousands are at work every day from four till eleven o'clock in the morning. It is surprising how much work has been done. The lines are extended almost from Cambridge to Mystic River so that very soon it will be morally impossible for the enemy to get between the works, except for one place which is supposed to be left purposely unfortified to entice the enemy out of their fortresses."

If Washington was hoping that the enemy would take the bait of attacking a purposely unfortified part of the American line to initiate a replay of Bunker Hill, he was to be sorely disappointed. William Howe was still recovering from the emotional trauma of the decimation of the British army during the attack on Breed's Hill and a sudden change of policy in London made him even less anxious to risk an all-out battle around Boston before he was massively reinforced. Lord North's original proposal to strip England of most of its infantry regiments in order to smash the American rebels before they could fully organize had been watered down by the cabinet to a more modest effort. The government would send five additional regiments from Ireland to America to enable Howe to initiate a limited offensive to push the rebels back from the immediate environs of Boston. However, Lord Dartmouth, who had authority over conduct of the war as Secretary of State for the colonies, vetoed even that limited operation and insisted that the reinforcements be re-routed to North Carolina to assist local Loyalists in holding that colony for the Crown.

The North Carolina operation turned out to be a fiasco, and both the king and Lord North decided it was time for a bolder direction of the colonial war. First minister and monarch agreed on a plan to replace Dartmouth, Lord North's half-brother, with the controversial Lord George Germain, who promised a more aggressive conduct of the war against the

American rebels. In a microcosm of the complexity and corruption of 18th-century British politics, North and George III bribed the incumbent holder of the title Lord of the Privy Seal to retire from his position in return for new titles and honors and an additional lifetime pension worth $250,000 a year in modern currency. Lord Dartmouth was then appointed Privy Seal, which maintained his seat in the cabinet, and Germain was brought in as Secretary of State for the American Colonies. Germain was experienced, aggressive, conceited, and vain, and promised his monarch that the pace of the war would almost immediately be accelerated. Former Massachusetts governor Thomas Hutchinson enthusiastically applauded Lord George's appointment. "I don't know of any person more to general satisfaction than Lord George Germain. He has the character of a great man." A junior cabinet minister noted, "his statements are the simplest and most unequivocal that could be made use of for his explaining opinions or dictating his interest." The absence of a specifically appointed commanding general of the British army meant that Germain, for better or worse, would direct military operations against the American rebels for most of the war and British hopes to retain their invaluable American colonies would ride on a man who had been sacked in disgrace from the British army and very nearly executed for cowardice.

Lord George Germain viewed British occupation of Boston as a strategic dead end that would interfere with his own pet concept of capturing New York and slicing the rebel provinces in two. Germain insisted that, "what has happened in New England I look upon as trifling when compared to the defection of New York. I often lamented Mr. Gage's drawing thence all his forces to Boston; as long as you maintained New York, the continent was divided. At present, there is free communication between all the disaffected colonials . . . until I see the post [New York] regained, I can see no prospect of ending this war with success."

Germain's preferred strategy would relegate Boston to a sideshow after Howe had safely pulled his army out of the city and transferred it to the environs of New York. Sir William would receive a large reinforcement in the spring of 1776, but the new troops would not be sent to Massachusetts; they were intended for Germain's New York campaign. The new cabinet minister expected these regiments to provide the overwhelming force necessary to crush the rebels in a single campaign and then force the defeated provincials to accept a compromise peace settlement before the French government was tempted to intervene and turn a colonial rebellion into a new European war. Germain was convinced that Boston was the wrong place to fight the decisive battle, for even if Howe was able to roll up the rebel flanks and capture their head-quarters in Cambridge, the colonials would simply melt back into the countryside and force the poorly adapted redcoats to engage in a running guerilla war that could drag on indefi-nitely.

The secondary role of the defense of Boston can be seen in Germain's planned deployment of reinforcements sched-uled to arrive in America between late 1775 and the spring of 1776. The garrison currently holding Boston would receive no infantry units and a paltry two batteries of Royal Artillery which would enable Howe to do little more than conduct a holding operation in Massachusetts. On the other hand, Sir Guy Carleton's army in Canada was scheduled to receive eight British infantry regiments and 5,000 Brunswick mercenaries in order to facilitate an invasion of the rebel provinces via Fort Ticonderoga and the Hudson River. Meanwhile, once Howe shifted his base from Boston to New York, he would have ac-cess to 12,000 Hessians, 3,500 Scottish Highlanders and 1,000 special volunteers from elite regiments stationed in England. The 3,500 men that Gage had commanded in the spring of 1775 were expected to increase almost 20-fold by the spring of 1776, as the two wings of the New York operation would employ over 55,000 men in the climax of a logistical effort that would have no parallel in Britain until the 20th century. All that Howe was expected to accomplish in Boston was to prevent the rebels from enjoying the sort of substantial victory that might spread the flames of rebellion before the gigantic British pincers squeezed the life out of the movement sometime during 1776.

American patriots from militia privates to George Washington were just as convinced as their British adversaries that the war would be decided in one campaign. Washington's letters to family and friends in the summer and early fall of 1775 indicate that he fully expected to be back in Mount Vernon by Christmas, and this attitude was shared by many of his subordinates. The reason for this optimism was not that the patriots dramatically underestimated the military potential of the motherland. They knew that Britain was probably the most powerful combination of naval and military power in the world. However, since most colonists were still primarily fighting to maintain their rights as British subjects, they expected that a solid show of force would convince the ministry to back down on its aggressive policies and return to the relationship between colonies and England that had existed before the Stamp Act crisis. After the effective showing made by the colonial forces at Concord and Bunker Hill, most Americans assumed that the advisors to King George would convince him to intervene directly, end taxation of the colonists and withdraw the British occupying force, which was still usually referred to as the "ministerial army" under the naive assumption that the monarch had not authorized their operations.

One of the first significant patriots to pull back from this optimistic scenario was Washington, who began accepting the possibility of a longer war sometime during the autumn of 1775. The Virginia general still hoped to gain a decisive victory over the British garrison in Boston, but he started to view such a victory more as a means of deflecting an eventual enemy blow at New York rather than forcing the ministry to end the war largely on American terms. The colonial commander was also becoming aware of a serious dilemma that faced him during the final months of the year. At present, he had enough infantry to offer some possibility of success in a properly coordinated offensive, but he had such limited artillery that the foot soldiers could not be properly supported. On the other hand, by the time substantial artillery reinforcements arrived, much or even most of the infantry might be long gone, as terms of enlistment expired with the beginning of the new year.

Much of the American military crisis in the autumn of 1775 can be attributed to the optimism of most colonials about the course of the war, combined with a traditional parsimony toward military spending in most provinces. When Massachusetts and the other New England colonies began shifting from dependence on short-term militiamen to a somewhat longer term provincial army in the wake of Lexington and Concord, the expectation was that the British government would come to its senses and enter serious negotiations before the end of the year. Therefore, dozens of provincial regiments were recruited on the basis of enlistment until January 1, 1776, with the Connecticut troops signed up for a period that was 30 days shorter than the other colonial forces. Most patriot leaders felt that raising a long-term army to fight a war that could not possibly last more than a few months was a waste of public funds. Even the somewhat more sophisticated John Adams insisted that the organization of a long-term professional army should be avoided at all costs and most fellow congressmen heartily agreed with his spirit of thrift in military affairs.

When Washington began to realize that the war would extend far into 1776 and perhaps much longer, he began to send alarming reports to congress asking for new recruits to replace the men who would be leaving on New Year's Day. Congress in turn sent Benjamin Franklin, Benjamin Harrison and Thomas Lynch to Cambridge to inspect the situation at close hand and to confer with the Virginian about the creation of a new Continental army. Washington insisted to his fellow congressmen that the only possible way to match British military power was to raise an army of at least 20,000 men enlisted for the duration of hostilities and supported by shorter-term provincial regiments that would be under each colony's control but available to supplement the Continental force in time of need. Considering the fact that the British government was preparing to deploy over 55,000 Regulars for the suppression of the rebellion, Washington's proposal was quite conservative. However, members of Congress still quaked at the very mention of a standing army and the most the general could accomplish was to gain approval to raise a new Continental army to be enlisted through 1776 with an agreement to reconsider the need for a longer-term force at the end of the upcoming campaign season. This short-sighted decision would ultimately give Washington the dubious distinction of watching his army virtually disintegrate in front of his eyes during two consecutive Decembers.

The threatened evaporation of the American army began to gain momentum on December 6, 1775, when the Connecticut regiments demanded an immediate cash bonus to remain in positions they were contracted to defend only until December 1. Washington met with the leaders of the Massachusetts Provincial Congress who agreed to loan the Virginian 3,000 provincial militia to man the lines until new units could be recruited. General Sullivan urged the New Hampshire Committee of Safety to rush 2,000 militiamen to help secure the rebel defenses as he insisted, "I hope the eager speed with which the New Hampshire forces will march to take possession of and defend our lines will convince the world of their love of liberty and regard to their country. As you find the business requires much infinite haste, I must entreat you not to give sleep to your eyes nor slumber to your eyelids until the troops are on the march." The New Hampshire patriots acted promptly on their general's request, and by December 18 Nathanael Greene noted the temporary solution to the crisis as the "Connecticut troops are gone home, the militia from this province and New Hampshire are come in to take their places. Upon this occasion they have discovered a zeal that does them the highest honor. New Hampshire behaves nobly."

The manpower shortage had been deferred for a few weeks, but Washington began to realize that the real crisis would occur on New Year's Day when the enlistments of virtually the whole army expired. The general, who would become a master of the art of reconstructing evaporating armies, initiated a number of important activities designed to ensure that the American lines were not found empty by the British on January 1, 1776. First, the number of regiments in the "Grand American Army" was reduced from 38 to 26 in order to avoid deploying skeleton units after a substantial number of men went home. Second, Washington realized that one of the best ways to entice men to sign on for an additional year was to allow them to serve with friends and neighbors commanded by officers familiar to them. Thus any person who re-enlisted was given a virtually free choice of regiment and company with incentives of a set of new clothes and a three-week furlough to sweeten the offer. Finally, junior officers were relieved of front line duties and sent to their hometowns to recruit new men from militia units that had been sent home after the first few days of the war. Of the 14,000 troops eligible to go home on New Year's Day, only about 7,500 men elected to sign up for an additional year. However, Washington's assignment of dozens of junior officers to local recruiting duties quickly began to pay dividends and the newly optimistic general admitted "the army is filling up. I think the prospect is better than it has been. Recruits come in out of the country plentifully, and the soldiers in the army begin to show a better disposition and to recruit cheerfully."

On January 1, 1776, a number of significant events occurred on both sides of the siege lines around Boston. Early that morning, just as thousands of colonial troops evacuated their lines and began the journey home, a British dispatch ship arrived in Boston Harbor with several documents for General Howe. The most important dispatch was a copy of King George's recent Proclamation of Rebellion. In his address to parliament, the king, whom most colonists expected to restrain the anti-American tendencies of the British ministers, essentially declared war on his provincial subjects and insisted that the rebels wanted to establish an "independent empire," a situation that he insisted he would resist to the death. Copies of the text of the proclamation were sent by flag of truce to Washington's headquarters and the general realized that the possibility of ending the war short of either independence or total submission was now quite bleak.

By a strange coincidence, just before the king's proclamation had been sent through the lines, a ceremony had been held at colonial army headquarters in which a new union flag

American floating battery from a British sketch. The sophisticated design and construction demonstrates the incredible ingenuity and industry of the colonists. Not clearly visible here, the ensign was of the "Appeal to Heaven" pattern.

of 13 stripes and a small inserted Union Jack was hoisted with cheers to the United Colonies of America. British observers in Boston could see the new flag with their telescopes, and they mistakenly assumed that the flag raising was in response to the arrival of the king's proclamation. The British Annual Register noted a few months later that "so great was the rage of indignation of the Americans at the king's speech, that they burnt the speech and changed their colors from a plain red emblem to a flag with 13 stripes as a symbol of the number and union of the colonies." A British lieutenant observing the Americans from Charlestown Peninsula reported, "a short time after they received the king's speech, they hoisted a union flag, their citadel fired 13 guns and gave a like number of cheers." Despite the enthusiasm for the new union emblem in the American lines, the rebel army was probably eminently beatable on that snowy New Year's afternoon. The drain of ended enlistments and promised furloughs reduced the force holding the provincial fortifications to only 5,600 men, a force only half as large as the army it besieged. However, no British unit stirred from its position during the day and as new recruits began to arrive in Cambridge, Washington immediately considered launching offensive operations.

On the morning of January 16, 1776, Washington called a council of war at his headquarters. The meeting included all senior American generals and two members of Congress, John

Adams and James Warren. The major topic of discussion was the commanding general's proposal to launch a surprise attack on the British as "it is indispensably necessary to make a bold attempt to conquer the ministerial troops in Boston before they are reinforced in the spring." The members of the council essentially supported Washington's plan with two significant provisos. First, over and above men returning from furloughs and new recruits coming in from the countryside, the American army should be augmented by at least 13 additional regiments of short term militiamen to serve from February 1 to March 31. Second, the attack would not take place until sufficient heavy artillery could be provided to offer some prospect of matching the British guns ringing Boston's defenses. While the individual colonial legislatures could easily draft additional infantry for short-term service, the far more substantial problem of securing artillery to counter the enemy cannon would be primarily solved by a rotund 25-year-old bookseller, who was at this moment orchestrating one of the most stupendous feats of logistics in the entire War of Independence.

During the British military occupation of Boston previous to Lexington and Concord, a favorite gathering place for bored Regular officers was Henry Knox's bookstore and café. The young bookseller quickly developed friendly relations with a number of His Majesty's officers and read virtually every military volume recommended by his new associates. When Knox abandoned Boston to volunteer for the colonial army, he brought with him invaluable knowledge concerning fortifications and artillery and immediately impressed Washington with his energy and intelligence. By November 1775 the new commander had limited Colonel Gridley's duties to chief engineer while Knox was installed as chief of artillery with a colonel's commission. About a week later, this appointment paid its first dividend when the former bookseller provided Washington with a bold plan to transport the invaluable heavy artillery currently stored at Fort Ticonderoga to the siege lines surrounding Boston. Knox proposed to take a small force to the recently captured fortress and select the most valuable guns from the post's numerous batteries. These cannon would then be transported by ox-driven wagons or sleds to Cambridge and provide the firepower necessary to blow the British out of Boston.

Washington, ever the gambler at heart, responded enthusiastically to his new artillery chief's proposal and drew up orders which instructed Knox to "immediately examine into the state of the artillery of this army and take an account of the cannon, mortars, shells, lead and ammunition that are wanting." The young colonel was then ordered to proceed to New York, "there to procure such of them as can possibly be had there." Knox was given wide-ranging powers to commandeer whatever stocks of artillery and ammunition were stored around New York City and then directed to secure the assistance of General Philip Schuyler in Albany to transport additional guns and equipment from Ticonderoga. He was also given $1,000 for expenses and a dispatch for Schuyler to provide whatever men or equipment might be needed to transport the guns back to Cambridge. Accompanied by his brother William and a single servant, Knox rode to New York City and immediately arranged for a number of cannon in that town to be dispatched to Cambridge. The young colonel then traveled north to Albany for a meeting with General Schuyler who, to his credit, proved extremely cooperative and offered Knox any equipment or men he needed. Soon dozens of colonial troops were accompanying the bookseller to the former British location of Fort Ticonderoga.

When Knox and his men arrived at the captured fort, Lake George was just beginning to freeze and the Americans worked against the clock to pry loose the most desirable guns from the fort's solid stone embrasures before the water route was closed to them. As icy winds ripped through the fortress, colonial soldiers used sledgehammers and chisels to free the invaluable guns from the iron bars and concrete emplacements which held them in position. This backbreaking labor produced 60 first-line guns including 43 cannon, 3 howitzers and 14 mortars with an aggregate weight of 120,000 pounds. Sixty tons of dead weight had to be dragged to the shore of the lake and loaded on an assortment of flatboats, barges and bateaux for the first leg of the journey to Cambridge. In addition to the guns, 30,000 musket flints, thousands of musket balls and hundreds of cannon balls were carefully packed in kegs for the trip to Massachusetts.

Henry Knox rode south to Fort George at the southern terminus of the lake to organize additional troops sent by General Schuyler while his brother William took charge of floating the boats down from Fort Ticonderoga. The vessels were so overloaded with guns and ammunition that water lapped within inches of their decks and a combination of sails and oars had to be employed to propel the sluggish craft southward. One boat ran aground and ripped out its bottom and the exhausted crew had to wade into icy water to remove the guns, push them onshore, repair the vessel and then repeat the loading process.

On December 15, 1775, the boats reached Fort George, and Henry Knox was waiting with 300 men and dozens of oxen and horse teams ready to draw 55 sledges south to Fort Edward, 10 miles away. By Christmas Day the long column had crossed the frozen Hudson River to the west shore in order to begin a march through Saratoga toward Albany. Each night the expedition would encamp with armed guards patrolling the animal enclosures while mounted patrols rode up and down the column of sleds which remained in the road for the night. The expedition reached Albany on January 4, 1776, just as a thaw set in and forced the anxious Knox to wait three days checking thermometers for signs of a renewed freeze. Finally, on January 7, a new coat of ice formed on the Hudson and hundreds of Albany citizens stood along the bank to cheer the sledge teams as they began to push across the river. One sled containing a huge 24-pounder broke through the ice near the Albany shore but dozens of civilians rushed out to help the soldiers retrieve the vital weapon.

As the artillery train neared the New York-Massachusetts border, a combination of deep snow and the rugged mountain passes of the Green Woods created a nightmare scene for the exhausted troops. Teamsters used long ropes tied to sleds

Henry Knox's men bring Ticonderoga's artillery to Boston, a 300-mile journey in the dead of winter.

and anchored to tree trunks to hold the guns in position while soldiers used blocks and tackles to ease each sleigh down the hills. Once the train crossed the wide but frozen Connecticut River, the New Yorkers left for home while a contingent of Massachusetts men stepped in to complete the journey. The weather continually deteriorated as the sleds pushed eastward, but Washington sent out hundreds of his own men to add muscle to the backbreaking labor of moving the guns. By the end of the first week of February, Knox was at Washington's headquarters with an impressive train of artillery and a bill for an additional $1,600 in expenses, a sum that the commanding general thought was well worth the cost. His new artillery commander had crossed 300 miles of wilderness, frozen lakes, almost impassable mountains and treacherous semi-frozen rivers to provide the American army with a major element of the military power needed to force the British out of Boston. As the newly-arrived cannon were polished and serviced by their enthusiastic gunners, George Washington was preparing to set in motion the daring plan designed to end the Boston campaign with an American victory.

Lord George Germain (1716-1785)

The single Englishman most responsible for the conduct of the war against the rebel colonists was George Sackville, Lord Germain. The Sackvilles were descended from Herbrand de Sackville, one of William the Conqueror's knights who was well rewarded for his activities in the battle of Hastings. His descendant, Thomas Sackville, was made Earl of Dorset by Queen Elizabeth I and given a huge mansion that had been occupied by the archbishop of Canterbury until the Reformation. On June 26, 1716, George Sackville was born in this 365-room mansion as the third son of an earl who was subsequently given the titles of Duke of Dorset, Knight of the Garter and Lord High Steward of Britain. Sackville's parents were close friends of King George II who became George's godfather while his godmother was Lady Betty Germain, the widow of one of the wealthiest men in England.

Sackville attended Westminster School and Trinity College, Dublin when his father became Lord Lieutenant of Ireland. The younger Sackville was viewed by fellow students as an arrogant, short-tempered person with a sloping forehead, dark complexion and large nose. At age 20 he entered the army as a captain in the Duke of Devonshire's Regiment, while the king made him a lieutenant colonel before his 25th birthday. He was seriously wounded at the battle of Fontenoy and was captured by the French, but his high social standing allowed him to recover from his wounds in the personal tent of the king of France. Later, Sackville participated in the battle of Culloden, won high praise from the commanding general, the Duke of Cumberland, and was subsequently elected to the House of Commons with a seat from Dover.

By the outbreak of the Seven Years War, George Sackville was the highest ranking field commander in the British army, but had developed running feuds with both the powerful Howe family and the leader of Britain's German allies, Prince Ferdinand. On August 1, 1759, at the battle of Minden, Prince Ferdinand, as senior officer of the allies, took command of all infantry units engaging the French while Sackville was placed in command of the cavalry. The allied infantry withstood four French assaults and initiated a counterattack with the expectation of immediate cavalry support. However, Sackville, in a gesture to show his hatred of Ferdinand, ignored orders to advance the horsemen for nearly 30 minutes, by which time the French had retreated into Minden's defenses, avoiding "the possible greatest defeat of the century against France" and permanently clouding the British general's reputation.

Prince Ferdinand, who was a cousin of George II, severely criticized his cavalry commander but issued no official censure. However, the prickly Sackville demanded a court martial to clear his name and a panel of British generals found him guilty of disobeying a superior officer and sentenced him to be shot. The king reduced the sentence to permanent expulsion from any service in His Majesty's forces, a punishment that was publicly read to every regiment in the British army. Sackville was also forbidden to ever again appear at court.

Sackville's apparently dead political and military career began to reverse itself after the death of George II and the coronation of George III. His wife, Lady Diana Sackville, set up a reconciliation for her husband with the new king, while Lady Betty Germain left him all of her lands and titles if he would assume the name of Germain. Thus when King George and Lord North realized that Lord Dartmouth was too mild a man to prosecute a war against the American rebels, they engineered a transfer of Dartmouth to Lord Privy Seal and installed Germain as Secretary of State for the Colonies, with responsibility for the prosecution of the war that would continue as long as North held the position of first minister. After his resignation in the wake of Yorktown, Germain was made Viscount Sackville by the king and died at his country estate in Sussex in 1785.

General Henry Knox (1750-1806)

Henry Knox was born on July 25, 1750, the seventh son of William Knox, a ship's captain and owner of a Boston wharf. When Henry was nine years old, his father sailed to the West Indies to collect money owed to him and died of disease while attempting to recover the funds. Knox was forced to leave Boston Latin School, where he was an excellent student, and become an apprentice bookseller. The future general made the best of the situation by a voracious reading of available military books which continued through his apprenticeship into his purchase of his own bookstore.

Knox grew into an imposing adult with a height of well over 6 feet and weighing over 250 pounds. His Boston bookstore quickly became a favorite meeting place for bored young British officers who readily discussed both society news and military tactics with the impeccably dressed American proprietor. The bookseller also developed a close relationship with Lucy Flucker, the daughter of one of the leading Tory families in Boston and the brother of a captain in the British army. After Knox rejected the Flucker family's offer of a regular army commission, the couple married against family wishes and escaped from Boston to Cambridge shortly before the battle of Bunker Hill.

Knox's military career took off with the arrival of George Washington, with whom he quickly developed a warm personal relationship and earned a high level of respect. After the Boston campaign, Knox was given a high degree of autonomy in the employment of his artillery corps, and his insistence on ferrying 18 artillery pieces across the ice-clogged Delaware River produced one of the key elements of victory in the American triumph at Trenton. After playing a key role in American successes at Monmouth and Yorktown, Knox became the youngest American-born major general in the Continental army.

After the War of Independence, Knox founded the controversial Society of the Cincinnati composed of former Continental officers, was appointed Secretary of War in the Articles of Confederation government and held the same post during

Washington's presidency. He actively supported the formation of a national military academy at West Point and proposed authorization of a national militia force called the National Guard. After exercising his final field command during the undeclared war with France in 1798, he returned to his estate in Maine where he choked to death on October 25, 1806.

CHAPTER XI

Climax at Dorchester Heights

*T*he arrival of Knox's artillery train and 13 additional regiments of short-term militia provided the opportunity for George Washington to plan the first major offensive of the Boston campaign. The activities of the recruiting officers in the country towns of New England had raised the strength of the 26 Continental regiments to nearly 14,000 men while the addition of the 60-day militia pushed the total strength of the army to over 20,000 troops, a situation that would be rarely repeated during most future campaigns. Washington was clearly tired of thinking only in defensive terms as he wrote Congress in February, "to have the eyes of a whole continent fixed with anxious expectation of hearing some great event, and to be restrained in every military operation is not very pleasing, especially as the means used to conceal my weaknesses from the enemy conceal it also from my friends and add to their wonder." Now the general had enough men and enough guns to turn from a holding action to an offensive and he had no intention of waiting until the traditional spring opening of the campaign season to implement a bold strike at the British.

On the other side of the siege lines, Sir William Howe was greatly annoyed at the Ministry's decision to redeploy the promised reinforcements from Ireland into operations in North Carolina. He noted sourly to his superiors, "with fewer troops, the success of any offensive operation will be very doubtful," and reminded the ministers that the rebels were not the country bumpkins portrayed in pro-government newspapers. "The American army is not in any way to be despised as it has in its ranks many European soldiers and all or most of the young men of spirit in the country, who are exceedingly diligent and attentive in their military profession." He also noted rather ominously, "the leaders of the rebels seem determined, since the receipt of the king's speech among them, to make the most diligent preparation for an active war and they will not retract until they have tried their fortunes in battle and are defeated."

While Howe had abandoned any hopes of offensive operations around Boston and was now thinking more in terms of evacuating to New York in the spring with as little enemy interference as possible, he still welcomed a rebel attack which he was sure would be annihilated by his better-trained soldiers. "I wish they would attempt so rash a step and quit those strong entrenchments to which they may attribute their present safety." Sir William was now determined to pull out of Boston but he much preferred the change of base to occur after he had won a significant battle over the colonials.

George Washington was preparing to give his adversary just such an opportunity, but not on the terms that Howe had envisioned. During the final days of February, colonial troops had been working diligently to strengthen key positions along the American lines in preparation for their commander's daring offensive. Washington wrote enthusiastically to Congress that, "we have, under many difficulties on account of hard, frozen ground, completed our work on Lechmere's Point. We have got some heavy pieces of ordnance placed there, two platforms fixed for mortars and everything for any offensive operations. Strong guards are now mounted there and at Cobble Hill." These activities were the prelude to the key operation of seizing Dorchester Heights in order to place Howe's army in an ultimately untenable position, as "I am preparing to take post on Dorchester Heights to try to see if the enemy will be so kind to come out to us. I should think if anything will induce them to hazard an engagement, it will be our attempting to fortify these heights, as, on that event's taking place, we shall be able to command a great part of the town and almost the whole harbor and to make them rather disagreeable than otherwise." As Washington wrote this confident letter, entrenching materials including "chandeliers," fascines and enormous quantities of hay were being collected; 2,000 bandages were being rolled; 45 bateaux, each capable of carrying 80 men, were constructed; and two floating batteries were assembled on the Charles River out of sight of British sentries.

Washington's operational plan was complex and quite risky but also generally well-conceived. First, the colonials would seize and fortify Dorchester Heights and construct fortifications to protect Knox's 24-pounders, which would command the harbor and threaten the Royal Navy vessels floating at anchor. Once the guns were fully operational, the provincials would seize a spur of Dorchester Heights called Nook's Hill. This promontory jutted out to within 600 yards of the British

Boston as it would have been seen by American gunners on Dorchester Heights. The Boston Tea Party took place at the right base of the hill in the middle distance.

lines on Boston Neck and the adjoining southern shoreline of Boston, and thus American artillery could command the entire rear of the redcoat line of fortifications. Washington and Horatio Gates had earlier made a careful survey of British emplacements and had noted the strategic importance of both Dorchester Heights and Nook's Hill, but had agreed that seizing the positions would be useless until they could be equipped with heavy artillery. The commanding general was genuinely surprised that neither Gage nor Howe had fully appreciated the importance of these positions and occupied them with redcoats, but now Washington was determined to make the British pay dearly for this oversight.

The most daring, and controversial, part of Washington's plan was a projected direct assault across the Charles River at the exact moment that Howe was fully committed to ejecting the rebels from Dorchester. As soon as the redcoats began climbing up the heights, two brigades of colonials under Generals Greene and Sullivan would be rowed across the river from Sewell's Point and Phipp's Farm in the newly-constructed barges. The Americans had enough vessels to ferry nearly 4,000 men in one crossing while two floating batteries mounting 24-pounders would provide direct artillery support for the colonial landing troops. Sullivan's brigade would land along Boston Common, seize the Powder House, Mount Horam and Beacon Hill, while one of Greene's regiments would land at Barton's Point, drive up Snow Street to capture the British batteries on Copp's Hill, while the rest of the brigade linked up with Sullivan's men to thrust down Orange Street toward Boston Neck. This combined force was expected to capture the British fortifications from the rear and allow American units deployed at Roxbury to pour into Boston and either annihilate or capture any part of the British garrison that was not already being decimated in its march up Dorchester Heights.

Washington was willing to take a daring gamble with the only significant military force in the rebel colonies since he did not wish merely to push the British out of Boston, but wanted to bag Howe's entire army in a spectacular triumph that might very well determine the outcome of the whole war.

While it appears that the general's official "family" of subordinate generals and staff members approved the risky plan, two of the most senior New England generals maintained then and later that the operation would result in disaster. Artemus Ward, still second in command of the army, argued vehemently that the American landing force would be chopped to pieces in the relatively confined space of Boston and that the loss of almost a third of the Continental army would then allow Howe to concentrate his forces on the surviving units and destroy them piecemeal. General William Heath was even more adamant in opposition to the Virginian's plan. "It would most assuredly produce only defeat and disgrace to the American army. The British general must be supposed to be a master of his profession; that, as such, he would first provide for the defense of the town, in every part, which was the sole deposit of all his stores; that when this was done, if his troops would afford a redundance sufficient for a sally, he might attempt it; but it is to be remembered that, at any rate, the town would be defended, and that it would be impossible for troops, armed and disciplined as the Americans were, to be pushed down in boats, at least one mile and a half open to the fire of all the British batteries on the west side of the town and the whole park of artillery, which might be drawn to the bottom of the Common long before the Americans could reach it . . . and that under such a tremendous fire, the troops could not effect a landing."

Heath's argument against the plan was sober and well thought out, but Washington was now convinced that he had already allowed opposition in councils of war to delay offensive operations on too many previous occasions. The commander was convinced that his plan would work and that a victory of annihilation over the British garrison in Boston might very well shock the British government into concessions that would give the colonists most of what they sought before the full weight of the vast British reinforcements could be used in an already probable New York campaign. Thus a major victory over the British in Massachusetts might make the Boston campaign the decisive, and essentially, only, major operation of the war. Washington was convinced that this might be the one and only time that he enjoyed a substantial numerical advantage over his opponent, and he had no intention of frittering away this opportunity. As he insisted to his troops, "every temporal advantage and comfort to us and our posterity depends upon the rigor of our exertions; in short, freedom or slavery must be the result of our conduct; there can therefore, be no greater inducement for men to behave well."

On Saturday, March 2, 1776, Sir William Howe was focusing his energy on drafting plans for a projected June evacuation of Boston while his officers were preparing for an upcoming masquerade and ball that was expected to be the social event of the season. However, soon after the sun set on a still, snowcovered landscape, the winter night's silence was shattered by a furious American bombardment as concealed guns emplaced on Cobble Hill, Lechmere's Point and Lamb's Dam near Roxbury opened fire simultaneously. Dozens of houses in Boston were badly damaged by the bombardment while half a dozen Regulars deployed in a regimental guardhouse became casualties when a shell landed in the building. Two 13-inch mortars, including one christened "Congress," and three 10-inch mortars were quickly engaged in a duel with British artillery that produced spectacular pyrotechnics. Abigail Adams, sitting in her bedroom 10 miles away in Braintree, provided her husband John with a dramatic account of the great artillery duel. "The house this instant shakes with the roar of cannon. I have been to the door and I find it a cannonade from our army. Orders, I find, are come, for all the remaining militia to repair to the lines Monday night by 12 o'clock. No sleep for me tonight!"

Just before dawn, Washington ordered a halt to the bombardment so that the invaluable big guns could be concealed from British counter-battery fire during the hours of daylight. However, at sundown on this March Sabbath, the guns were trundled back into position and the bombardment began anew. Abigail Adams, now a seasoned spectator of artillery duels, climbed to the top of Penn's Hill to watch the new installment of the cannonade. When she returned home well after mid-

Abigail Adams left behind the most vivid eyewitness account of the bombardment of Boston from Dorchester Heights.

night, the bombardment was still going at full intensity. She insisted to her husband in Philadelphia, "the sound, I think, is one of the grandest in nature and is one of the true species of the 'sublime.' I could no more sleep than if I had been in the engagement; the rattling of the windows, the jar of the house, the constant roar of the twenty-four pounders and the bursting of the shells gives us such ideas and we realize a scene of which we could scarcely form any conception. I hope to give you joy of Boston, even if it is in ruins, before I send this away."

Soon after sundown on Monday, March 4, the American guns opened a third bombardment, but this time the initial shots were followed by the movement of infantry forces. Using the artillery duel for cover, an advance force of 800 riflemen marched up the narrow road that led to Dorchester Heights. Each man was cradling a Pennsylvania long rifle in his arms and within an hour these elite troops had set up positions on Nook's Hill and along the eastern part of Dorchester Heights overlooking Castle William. Although the night was clear and cold, the Heights were shrouded in a low-level fog which provided perfect cover from British observation. As soon as the riflemen had established a security screen, an additional 1,200 Continentals under General Thomas started up the hill. These men were accompanied by a long train of horse- and ox-drawn wagons loaded with entrenching tools and construction materials. As the carts moved up the hill, men placed a wall of twisted hay between the vehicles and the British lines to muffle the sound of creaking wheels. Just as the American guns reached a crescendo, Thomas' men deployed into small units and listened intently to the instructions of Colonel Gridley concerning the type of fortifications he wanted to be constructed.

The chief engineer marked out a long saddle along Dorchester Heights and ordered one redoubt constructed on the eastern end of the ridge while an even larger fortification was to be erected nearest Nook's Hill. These two forts would serve as anchors for a long, 10-foot parapet in between. Since the ground was frozen to a depth of 18 inches, Gridley ordered the construction of dozens of devices called chandeliers, heavy wood frames in which fascines could be stretched and then held in place by stakes while being covered with dirt. This technique worked well, and by 4 A.M. Tuesday morning, a formidable line of fortifications had been erected in a feat of construction about which General Heath noted, "never was so much work done in so short a space of time."

Just as Thomas' men were ready to drop from sheer exhaustion, 3,000 reinforcements arrived on the heights and relieved the working party. This larger force quickly covered the chandeliers with frozen earth and sod and completed a series of massive walls that were almost impervious to musket fire. Selected detachments hurried into neighboring orchards and cut down dozens of trees, sharpened their trunks, and started placing abatis in front of the walls to discourage a prompt British infantry attack. Meanwhile, former Boston merchant William Davis had convinced Washington to deploy dozens of heavy barrels filled with earth and rocks around the base of the parapet at the edge of a steep cliff below. These objects appeared from a distance to simply be the forward edge of the entrenchments; in reality, they were designed to be rolled down the hill toward any approaching redcoats who would theoretically be injured or killed by the velocity of the objects.

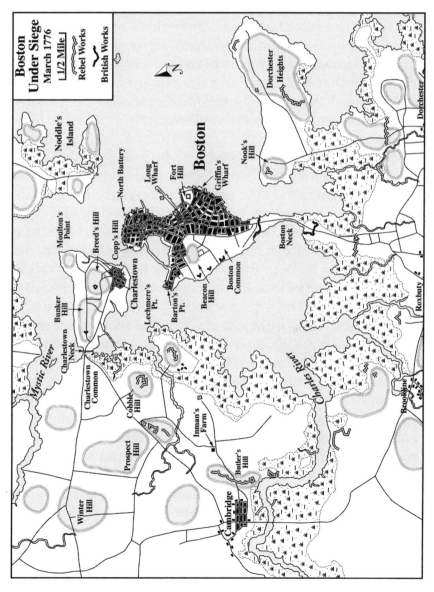

Tuesday, March 5, was the sixth anniversary of the Boston Massacre, and dawn of that day revealed to the shocked British officers the real purpose of the American bombardment. One stunned redcoat officer noted, "the rebel fortifications were raised with an expedition equal to that of the genie belonging to Aladdin's wonderful lamp." Even Howe complemented his adversaries as he noted, "the rebels have done more in one night than my whole army would have done in a month. It must have been the employment of at least twelve thousand men." Admiral Shuldham, newly-appointed commander of Royal Navy forces in the colonies, emphasized to Sir William that the fleet could not remain in Boston unless the Americans were dislodged from Dorchester Heights and Howe reluctantly admitted that the army was as insecure as the naval vessels. However, Sir William had a strong sense of both personal and national honor and he realized that he commanded a force that British ministers, military colleagues and Americans loyal to the king assumed was large enough to defeat almost any rebel force that could be arrayed against it. He had excellent officers, well-trained men, a powerful train of artillery and substantial naval support; to give up the city that had been the symbol of British military presence in America for the last several years without an attempt to defeat the rebels besieging it would be a disgrace to his reputation and that of his army. Therefore, rather than submit to such an indignity, he would risk virtually his whole army in a supreme effort to gain control of Dorchester Heights and, hopefully, drive the rebel army back into the countryside in order to allow the British army to shift its base from Boston to New York on Howe's own terms.

Sir William's operational plan was to order General Hugh Percy to select 2,400 of his best men, have them rendezvous at Castle William out in Boston Harbor and prepare for a night assault on the new American position. The 40th, 44th, 49th, 52nd and 55th regiments of foot were marched to Long Wharf and supplied with one day's rations and a canteen filled with water and rum. The men had been specifically forbidden to load their weapons in favor of a bayonet attack that would receive extensive artillery support from both shore batteries and naval vessels. The assault force would be landed at high tide along the base of Dorchester Heights and, using the cover of darkness and immense artillery support, would sprint up toward the rebel fortification. Howe had bitter memories of the impact of colonial fire on his overloaded troops climbing Breed's Hill and he was not about to repeat that scenario. This time, his assault force would leave behind its heavy packs and other encumbrances and use speed and the cover of night to slam into the rebel defenders before they could decimate the attackers. If all went well, by Wednesday morning the British army would hold Dorchester Heights and the mauled American defenders would be fortunate to be hanging on to their lines in Cambridge.

Howe had learned from his experiences at Bunker Hill, but he was unable to screen the mobilization of his assault force from colonial lookouts, and Washington immediately responded to Sir William's challenge. The Virginian was determined to spare no effort to make the fortifications on Dorchester Heights invulnerable to attack and quickly dispatched an additional 2,000 men to reinforce the garrison. By nightfall on March 5 the Dorchester lines were crammed with 5,000 Continentals and 800 riflemen. Washington encouraged the already confident defenders by noting, "remember, it is the 5th of March and it is time to avenge the death of your brethren."

Meanwhile, Washington's own assault force of 4,000 men was under parade at Cambridge ready to make an attack across the Charles River. Each general, without realizing it, was about to throw an attack force against a force of defenders that outnumbered its adversary and was entrenched in almost impenetrable fortifications. Even when Howe decided at the last moment to reinforce his assault unit with 1,100 additional grenadiers and light infantry, his men would be facing a garrison almost twice its size, while the colonials led by Sullivan and Greene would be encountering a force of redcoat defenders that outnumbered them three to two and was supported by the most powerful artillery batteries in the city. Thus on this frigid, gloomy Tuesday afternoon, two powerful traps had been put in place and conditions were ripe for what might develop into the bloodiest single day of the entire American Revolution.

Each general relished the idea of a decisive confrontation against his opponent whatever the risk this might entail, but as the British Regulars were rowed out to Castle William in preparation for their night assault, the weather began to deteriorate rapidly. A driving wind swept in from the sea accompanied by sheets of rain, a condition which threatened to swamp the relatively fragile British support vessels *Sea Venture*, *Venus*, *Spy* and *Success*. On Dorchester Heights the defenders covered themselves and their muskets with blankets or sheets of canvas while they waited out the storm near cannons loaded with grapeshot and trained on the possible British landing points. While the storm swept through Boston shattering sheds and fences and blowing down some houses, the redcoat assault troops were stranded at Castle William. Most Massachusetts natives rated the storm as the worst to hit the area since the early 1750's and by midnight Howe was forced to cancel the operation for at least 24 hours.

Wednesday morning dawned just as stormy as the night before and both generals began to order the assault troops to stand down. The storm finally began to abate on Thursday afternoon and Howe began to consider the possibility of a Friday night attack, but Admiral Shuldham convinced Sir William that the delay had allowed the rebels to range their artillery batteries directly on the British fleet and warned the general that naval support was now out of the question. The British commander was caught in a brutal quandary: to remain in Boston was to expose the army to imminent destruction; to withdraw would guarantee a substantial loss of supplies and equipment and provide the rebels with a major psychological victory.

When General Howe called a council of war to discuss the increasingly distasteful options, his subordinate officers agreed that the most important priority was to save the army at whatever cost; equipment could be replaced, trained Regulars could not. Sir William was more than a little embarrassed that he had recently insisted to his superiors that he could hold Boston indefinitely; now he would have the unpleasant task of informing the ministry that the rebels had pushed him out of "invulnerable" fortifications. Howe's only consolation was that an early evacuation of Boston might allow him to initiate an accelerated timetable for the capture of New York, a prize that seemed much more important to King George and Lord Germain. Thus with more than a little trepidation, the general reluctantly gave the order for the vaunted British army to evacuate its main base in the American colonies.

The "mortifying" evacuation of Boston began on Sunday, March 10, when all sick and wounded troops were loaded on transports while all able-bodied men were ordered to send their bedding and knapsacks to the wharves for imminent loading. All stores that sold liquor were shut down to prevent drunken soldiers from looting, and anyone found selling spirits was to be arrested and his wares immediately destroyed. Rum that could not be loaded on transports was destroyed by provost marshals. Heavy artillery was dismantled and stored on ships whenever possible or thrown into the harbor if space was not available. Ammunition was removed from magazines and carted to the wharves while grenadiers and light infantrymen were released from all garrison duties and used to supervise the loading of ships.

The pace of the British evacuation appeared simultaneously leisurely and frenzied as Howe tried to maintain the facade that this was a totally voluntary change of base while he peered warily at the American guns frowning down on the city. The general's trump card was that he was evacuating a city that his adversaries considered sympathetic to the rebel cause. He immediately warned Boston's civilian officials that he would burn the city to the ground if the colonial forces made any attempt to interfere with operations. When the city selectmen sent a letter to Washington with this information, the American commander was caught in a complex dilemma of military protocol. The fact that the British commander made no attempt to contact his American counterpart directly as one general to another rankled at a man who had been snubbed often by His Majesty's officers during his service with the Virginia provincial army. Since 18th-century generals fighting in European campaigns constantly demonstrated courtesy and deference to their opposing counterparts, Howe's implication that Washington was nothing more than the chieftain of a band of unwashed insurrectionists was an intolerable insult. Ultimately, Washington compromised by ordering his men to continue preparations for a possible assault on the British army while refraining from actually firing on the redcoats as long as it appeared they were withdrawing from Boston. The Virginian could console himself with the knowledge that even though he was addressed as *Mister* Washington by his adversaries, those same opponents were nonetheless essentially retreating due to his bold and successful gamble to fortify Dorchester Heights.

While British troops launched occasional forays against exposed American positions and British artillery initiated occasional bombardments, the redcoat supply officers loaded horses on ships, smashed gun carriages, tossed cannon and cannon balls into the water and supervised the loading of excess rations. Although patriot households endured some level of looting and destruction from the retreating Regulars, the most panic-stricken residents of the city were the Loyalists who feared imminent retaliation for their attachment to British rule. These "friends of government" were determined to avoid the questionable mercies of their patriot adversaries, and Howe quickly found himself inundated with Tory requests for space on his transports. Since the British government had specifically ordered the general to evacuate any Loyalist who wished to leave Boston, huge amounts of equipment had to be destroyed or left behind in order to accommodate the terrified civilians and their considerable baggage.

On Thursday, March 14, the streets of Boston were barricaded as the British army began to contract its lines and Washington began to suspect that the evacuation might actually be a gigantic ruse designed to allow Howe to land somewhere below the city and outflank the American lines. The next day

The British evacuate Boston on March 17, 1776.

the colonial commander ordered Colonel Knox to significantly reinforce the artillery batteries on Nook's Hill to parry any surprise British flanking attack. However, the lines remained relatively quiet both Friday and Saturday and as Sunday dawned, the final act in the drama of the Boston campaign began. At 4 A.M. on this frigid St. Patrick's Day, the remaining units of the British garrison were lined up along the city wharves and given final rations before being loaded on transports. Five hours later, redcoats deployed on Bunker Hill marched down the slopes toward embarkation sites. Then the light infantry and grenadiers guarding Boston Neck were pulled back to the harbor area. The withdrawal proceeded with no hindrance on the part of the Americans. As one British officer noted, "although we kept a constant fire of twenty-four pounders, our troops did not receive the smallest molestation, they did not return a single shot." This participant insisted that it was fortunate that the rebels did not interfere as Howe was not bluffing about burning the town. "I am informed everything was prepared to set the town in a blaze had they fired one cannon."

The British fallback encouraged the colonial forces to initiate a cautious advance toward the city. Two men sent forward to reconnoiter the strength of the remaining British troops deployed on Bunker Hill reported back to their regimental commander that the "Regulars" guarding the hill were actually mannequins dressed in red coats. Artemus Ward, Colonel Ebenezer Learned, and about 500 men from Roxbury knocked down the barricade at Boston Neck and pushed their way through a parting gesture from the British, hundreds of "crow's feet," small iron balls studded with inch long sharp points that had at least one side upraised no matter which way they were dropped. General Israel Putnam led a detachment further into the town and "in the name of the United Colonies of North America" took possession of "all the fortresses of this large and once flourishing metropolis, which the flower of the British army, headed by an experienced general and supported by a formidable fleet of men-of-war, had but an hour before evacuated in the most precipitous and cowardly manner."

Boston was now free of redcoats but was still plagued by a smallpox outbreak and Washington quashed any idea of a full-scale victory parade and sent only a token force of 500 men who had already survived the disease to take possession of the city. By March 23 the town selectmen assured the American commander that the city was now safe to enter and on that Wednesday afternoon, the main body of the American army marched into Boston. One eyewitness noted, "while marching through the streets, the inhabitants appeared at their doors and windows; though they manifested a lively joy at being liberated from their long confinement, they were not altogether free from a melancholy gloom which ten tedious months siege has spread over their faces." The British fleet was still lingering offshore waiting for orders to proceed to Halifax, Nova Scotia to refit for the upcoming New York campaign. The Royal Navy transports were loaded to capacity with 9,000 soldiers, 2,000 seamen and Royal Marines, and over 1,000 Loyalists.

Finally, on March 27 the order to set sail was given and the fleet disappeared over the horizon.

On April 4, 1776, George Washington made the short ride from his headquarters in Cambridge to the center of Boston and received a hero's welcome from the largely patriot inhabitants. While the general was still disappointed that he had not annihilated Howe's army, his mood was brightened considerably when his quartermasters completed an inventory of captured equipment that included over 100 pieces of artillery, several auxiliary naval vessels, thousands of musket balls, and enormous quantities of food, all of which would be invaluable assets in the battle for New York which now seemed imminent. Three thousand miles away and several weeks later, the Duke of Manchester rose in the House of Lords and summarized the results of the Boston campaign to his fellow peers of the realm. "The army of Britain, equipped with every possible essential of war; a chosen army with chosen officers; backed by the power of a mighty fleet, has for many tedious months

The Revolution comes full circle. Howard Pyle's impression of the reading of the Declaration of Independence in Boston in July, 1776. The artist has carefully aligned the buildings to evoque Paul Revere's engraving of the Boston Massacre six years earlier.

been imprisoned within Boston by the Provincial army who with their watchful guards, permitted no inlet to the country; now, British generals whose names never met with a blot of dishonour are forced to quit that town which was the first object of the war, the immediate cause of hostilities, the place of arms which has cost this nation more than a million pounds to defend." A largely amateur force of American colonists had proven time and again over the previous year that they were capable of frustrating the best plans of the most powerful military force of their time. British armies might experience a number of spectacular victories during the next five years, but the feeling of confidence instilled in many Americans by the train of events from Lexington and Concord through Bunker Hill and culminating in the British evacuation of Boston would continue to haunt the British military effort in America right up to the final surrender outside the village of Yorktown.

Impact of the Campaign

The outcome and impact of the Boston campaign was debated in both the American colonies and the British motherland and continues to provoke discussion today. While the overall casualties for the year-long campaign were relatively modest by Civil War and World War standards, the percentage of killed and wounded as part of the total number of troops available was far from insignificant, especially on the redcoat side.

The Boston campaign resulted in just over 1,500 British casualties, about one-seventh of the forces deployed in Massachusetts during 1775-1776. This total included slightly more than 300 British troops killed, about 300 men wounded severely enough to put them permanently out of the army, and about 900 soldiers who eventually returned to active service. Most significantly, nearly 25 percent of the British officer corps in America was either dead or permanently incapacitated during the campaign, a staggering blow to an army that had no reserve pool of well-trained officers readily available to replace these losses. A significant number of the most talented, energetic junior officers in His Majesty's service were lost to the British army for the remainder of the war.

On the other hand, American losses during the campaign were a relatively modest 600 men, about 2 percent of the colonials who were listed on active duty muster rolls at some point during the year. The total list of 200 killed, 30 captured and 270 wounded represented a permanent loss of about 300 men to the provincial cause, a fairly modest figure considering the pool of able bodied men available to the rebellious colonies at this time.

The most significant engagement of the campaign, the battle of Bunker Hill, was ultimately one of the bloodiest days of the entire war for the British army. The 226 battle deaths suffered by the redcoats on June 17, 1775, was never exceeded for the remainder of the war and was 40 to 50 men higher than comparable battles such as Monmouth, Freeman's Farm and Brandywine. The total casualty list of 1,054 was the largest tally of killed and wounded of the entire war and was only less of a catastrophe than Saratoga and Yorktown because virtually no redcoats were captured. On the other hand, the provincial total of 140 fatalities was substantially exceeded by colonial losses at Long Island, Brandywine, Germantown and Monmouth, all of which resulted in approximately 200 battle deaths. The total of just over 450 killed, wounded and captured on Charlestown Peninsula was exceeded a number of times during the course of the war and was dwarfed by the 6,000 casualties at Charleston five years later.

An analysis of casualties inflicted versus losses incurred during the Boston campaign reveals a clear-cut victory for the American rebels over the British Regulars. However, the psychological impact of the campaign was probably an even more one-sided colonial triumph. While both Thomas Gage and William Howe consistently underplayed the seriousness of their setbacks during the campaign, and Howe insisted that the "real" battle would be fought in New York, the impact of a forced evacuation of the largest city in New England due to the tactical success of an amateur army of "country people" was enormous.

The evacuation itself was almost bloodless and the British army remained intact, but the redcoats left behind large quantities of weapons and equipment after failing to decisively defeat the rebels at any point during the previous year. The result of this evacuation was that by late March of 1776 the 13 rebellious provinces were at least temporarily free of any significant British military presence within their borders. They had gained a vital window of opportunity that would allow them to set up a functioning independent government with a corresponding Declaration of Independence before the British army and navy could fully suppress these actions.

Thus the Boston campaign could reasonably be selected as one of the four decisive campaigns of the entire War of Independence, along with the re-igniting of a dying cause at Trenton and Princeton, the first capitulation of a major British army at Saratoga, and the climactic surrender of Cornwallis at Yorktown. In many respects, while the war would continue to drag on for another seven years, the British cause would never totally recover from the psychological impact of their failure to crush the American rebels before they could fully organize to resist the imperial forces on a long-term basis.

Order of Battle

Battle of Bunker Hill

Unit strength in parenthesis followed by casualties

British Army
General William Howe (3,000 men)

4th Regiment of Foot (79 men)

Grenadier Company
Light Infantry Company

Killed		Wounded	
1	Sergeant	1	Sergeant
13	Rank and File	1	Drummer
4	Officers	29	Rank and File

Total 49 casualties

5th Regiment of Foot (308 men)

Grenadier Company
Light Infantry Company
8 Battalion Companies

Killed		Wounded	
22	Rank and File	8	Officers
		10	Sergeants
		2	Drummers
		110	Rank and File

Total 152 casualties

10th Regiment of Foot (72 men)
Grenadier Company
Light Infantry Company

Killed		*Wounded*	
2	Sergeants	6	Officers
5	Rank and File	1	Drummer
		39	Rank and File

Total 53 casualties

18th Regiment of Foot (72 men)
Grenadier Company
Light Infantry Company

Killed		*Wounded*	
3	Rank and File	1	Officer
		7	Rank and File

Total 11 casualties

22nd Regiment of Foot (74 men)
Grenadier Company
Light Infantry Company

Killed	
1	Officer

23rd Regiment of Foot (70 men)
Grenadier Company
Light Infantry Company

Killed		*Wounded*	
2	Sergeants	4	Officers
1	Drummer	2	Sergeants
11	Rank and File	1	Drummer
		35	Rank and File

Total 56 casualties

35th Regiment of Foot (78 men)
Grenadier Company
Light Infantry Company

Killed		*Wounded*	
1	Officer	4	Officers
18	Rank and File	3	Sergeants
		2	Drummers
		41	Rank and File

Total 69 casualties

38th Regiment of Foot (336 men)

Grenadier Company
Light Infantry Company
8 Battalion Companies

Killed		Wounded	
1	Officer	8	Officers
2	Sergeants	4	Sergeants
23	Rank and File	1	Drummer
		69	Rank and File

Total 108 casualties

43rd Regiment of Foot (313 men)

Grenadier Company
Light Infantry Company
8 Battalion Companies

Killed		Wounded	
2	Sergeants	4	Officers
23	Rank and File	4	Sergeants
		1	Drummer
		69	Rank and File

Total 103 casualties

47th Regiment of Foot (285 men)

Grenadier Company
Light Infantry Company
8 Battalion Companies

Killed		Wounded	
2	Officers	5	Officers
2	Sergeants	3	Sergeants
15	Rank and File	47	Rank and File

Total 74 casualties

52nd Regiment of Foot (299 men)

Grenadier Company
Light Infantry Company
8 Battalion Companies

Killed		Wounded	
4	Officers	6	Officers
1	Sergeant	7	Sergeants
20	Rank and File	73	Rank and File

Total 111 casualties

59th Regiment of Foot (71 men)

Grenadier Company
Light Infantry Company

Killed		Wounded	
1	Officer	25	Rank and File
6	Rank and File		

Total 32 casualties

63rd Regiment of Foot (78 men)

Grenadier Company
Light Infantry Company

Killed		Wounded	
1	Officer	20	Officers
1	Sergeant	2	Sergeants
7	Rank and File	1	Drummer
		25	Rank and File

Total 57 casualties

65th Regiment of Foot (78 men)

Grenadier Company
Light Infantry Company

Killed		Wounded	
1	Officer	5	Officers
1	Sergeant	1	Sergeant
8	Rank and File	1	Drummer
		25	Rank and File

Total 42 casualties

1st Battalion of Royal Marines (346 men)

Killed		Wounded	
4	Officers	4	Officers
2	Sergeants	2	Sergeants
15	Rank and File	55	Rank and File

Total 82 casualties

2nd Battalion of Royal Marines (357 men)

Killed		Wounded	
2	Officers	3	Officers
5	Rank and File	1	Sergeant
		29	Rank and File

Total 40 casualties

Detachment of Royal Artillery Regiment (Approx. 100 men)

Wounded

30 Officers
2 Sergeants
8 Rank and File

Total 40 casualties

NOTE: Of the 3,000 men under Howe's command approximately 2,200 actually participated in the assault with the remaining companies serving in a primarily reserve capacity

Total reported British losses

Killed		*Wounded*	
1	Lieutenant Colonel	3	Majors
2	Majors	27	Captains
8	Captains	32	Lieutenants
10	Lieutenants	8	Ensigns
15	Sergeants	40	Sergeants
1	Drummer	12	Drummers
191	Rank and File	706	Rank and File

Provincial Army
General Israel Putnam, Colonel William Prescott, Colonel John Stark
(6,400 men)

Regiment of William Prescott (Massachusetts)

10 Companies (456 men)

Killed	*Wounded*
43	46

Total 89 casualties

Regiment of James Frye (Massachusetts)

10 Companies (493 men)

Killed	*Wounded*	*Missing*
10	38	4

Total 52 casualties

Regiment of Ebenezer Bridge (Massachusetts)
7 Companies (315 men)

Killed	Wounded
17	25

Total 42 casualties

Regiment of Moses Little (Massachusetts)
10 Companies (400 men)

Killed	Wounded
7	23

Total 30 casualties

Regiment of Ephraim Doolittle (Massachusetts)
7 Companies (308 men)

Killed	Wounded
6	9

Total 15 casualties

Regiment of Samuel Gerrish (Massachusetts)
8 Companies (421 men)

Killed	Wounded
3	5

Total 8 casualties

Regiment of Thomas Gardner (Massachusetts)
10 Companies (425 men)

Wounded
7

Regiment of Artemus Ward (Commanded by Lieutenant Colonel Jonathan Ward) (Massachusetts)
9 Companies (449 men)

Killed	Wounded
1	6

Total 7 casualties

Regiment of Jonathan Brewer (Massachusetts)
8 Companies (318 men)

Killed	Wounded
12	22

Total 34 casualties

Regiment of John Nixon (Massachusetts)
3 Companies (224 men)
Killed
3

Regiment of Benjamin Woodbridge (Massachusetts)
8 Companies (379 men)
Wounded
8

Regiment of Asa Whitcomb (Massachusetts)
10 Companies (470 men)

Killed	*Wounded*	*Missing*
5	8	2

Total 15 casualties

Regiment of John Stark (New Hampshire)
10 Companies (Approx. 500 men)

Killed	*Wounded*
15	45

Total 60 casualties

Regiment of James Reed (New Hampshire)
10 Companies (486 men)

Killed	*Wounded*	*Missing*
3	29	1

Total 33 casualties

Regiment of Israel Putnam (Connecticut)
10 Companies (Approx. 500 men)
No casualties

Regiment of Joseph Spencer (Connecticut)
2 Companies (120 men)

Killed	*Wounded*
20	29

Total 49 casualties

Artillery Regiment of Richard Gridley (Massachusetts)
3 Companies (133 men)
Wounded
4

NOTE: Returns of regiments involved place just under 6,400 men in the vicinity of the battle between Charlestown Common and Breed's Hill; approximately 2,000 men took an active part in the battle with a loss of 145 killed and missing, and 304 wounded.

Index

Index

Index